HOW TO RECRUIT

Hire and Retain
Great People

Also by Kerry Johnson

New Mindset, New Results

*Why Smart People Make Dumb Mistakes
With Their Money*

Willpower

Mastering Self-Confidence with NLP

Phone Sales

Sales Magic

How to Read Your Client's Mind

Peak Performance

Trust-Based Selling

The Referral Mindset

Mastering the Virtual Sale

Negotiating the Deal

HOW TO
RECRUIT

Hire and Retain
Great People

Kerry Johnson MBA, Ph.D.

MEDIA

Published 2022 by Gildan Media LLC
aka G&D Media
www.GandDmedia.com

FIRST EDITION 2022

Front cover design by David Rheinhardt of Pyrographx

Interior design by Meghan Day Healey of Story Horse, LLC

Library of Congress Cataloging-in-Publication Data is available upon request

ISBN: 978-1-7225-0177-8

10   9   8   7   6   5   4   3   2   1

Contents

Introduction

Have you ever hired someone who didn't work out? Ever spend months interviewing candidates and at the end just guessed at whom to pick? And the worst: have you ever spent weeks interviewing and still couldn't find the right person? You are probably like a lot of leaders I work with, who want to pick the right people without spending a lot of time searching.

A good economy means a lower unemployment rate. With fewer people looking for jobs, getting good people is all the more difficult. In 2019, the unemployment rate went down to 3.5 percent across America. Certain states had even fewer job openings. In fact, it was so difficult to find good people that many employers found themselves in bidding wars to attract talent. The worst part is the desperation of not being able to grow your business because you can't find good people.

One financial advisor in Cleveland, Ohio, searched for an assistant for more than a year. He thought he found a good administrative candidate, a fellow Marine; they met at a military club. He recruited her from a job she was not enamored with. (We will discuss later why recruiting those already employed is the easiest and best way of hiring good candidates.) She worked effectively for about six months. But then decided to spend the rest of her preretirement as a volunteer. Now the financial advisor is back searching for another candidate.

A few years ago, the same advisor recruited a recent college graduate. He paid for licensing and even six months of training. The new hire lasted only six months past the training investment. Once again, the hire was a waste of time. If this Cleveland financial advisor knew what you are about to learn, he would have saved nearly three years of hiring mistakes. He would have been able to turn his focus to increasing sales instead of spinning his wheels recruiting staff.

The Great Resignation

During the pandemic of 2020, more than 22 million jobs were lost. But after the Covid Omicron variant, many of those who worked before the lockdowns across the United States decided to retire or resign—a phenomenon labeled the "Great Resignation." Two years after Covid induced massive job losses, more than 10.6 million jobs remained unfilled. Unemployment decreased from 14.8 percent during the pandemic to only 3.9 percent after. Every employer continues to struggle to find workers in a dwindling pool of available candidates. As late as December 2021, payrolls remained 3.6 million jobs shy of the high employment levels of February 2020.

Because of increased savings accumulated during Covid, many workers over the age of fifty-five decided to leave the workforce.

Labor force participation had been decreasing 0.3 percent per year. But the decreasing amount of people willing to work dropped even more in 2022. In fact, 3.3 million people retired soon after 2020. The Federal Reserve reported that retirements included 2.4 million more people than expected based on demographics alone.

But there is worse news. According to a recent Stanford University study, 3 million of those already out of work between the ages of twenty and sixty-five will stay out of the workforce indefinitely. This is called *long social distancing*. These workers tend to be women, lack a college degree, and have worked in low-paying jobs. These workers have made changes in their employment outlook to accommodate a permanent departure from the workforce.

Emblematic of the trend toward either a delayed reentry into or permanent departure from the workforce is an orthopedic physician friend in his late sixties. Greg had a great practice for nearly forty years before Covid. Because of the lockdowns and the prohibition against elective surgeries, his practice stalled. Staff were in short supply for many weeks. He and his partners paid the salaries of those who remained for many months out of savings. This was unsustainable. Eventually, Greg decided that retirement was better than bleeding his IRA for business-related expenses. Greg would rather have continued his practice. He enjoyed his career. Instead, he became a statistic.

Many members of the Great Resignation between the ages of twenty-four and fifty-four will make their way back into the workforce as their savings dwindle. But it may take a few years. There are many reasons for this delay. Over 13 million households have young children. Many schools have been slow to reopen, forcing families to find expensive childcare or provide it themselves, causing them to stay out of the workforce.

The worst time of the stay-at-home trend was in January 2022, when 9 million people reported Covid illnesses. They unable to work anyplace and stayed home, even without symptoms. As many return to the workforce, they will turn to gig jobs as a stepping-stone to more formal work environments.

All of these are reasons for wage inflation and enhanced benefits as companies compete for very few workers. This has also caused a wage-feedback loop. As wages increase for scarce workers, companies increase prices. This inflation in turn diminishes wages, creating a demand for still higher pay. To make matters worse, birthrates have been decreasing, making the workforce of the future even smaller. To fill the gap, many companies engaged temporary and seasonal workers. But even this pool of workers proved hard to find as borders shut down.

All of this means that your selection and sourcing skills will be put to the test. No longer can you wait for workers to appear when you have an opening. No longer will you have multiple candidates to choose from. The need to be proactive in sourcing workers is greater now than before the Great Resignation. Finding good people will continue to be increasingly challenging.

The Great Retirement

The number of workers retiring has been on a steady pace since World War II. Because of the stellar returns of a bull market, many seniors, even under the age of sixty-five, had enough money saved that work no longer appealed to them. The labor force decreased steadily by 0.3 percent for the last fifty years.

Since the pandemic began, 3.3 million people have retired. According to the St. Louis Federal Reserve, that is 2.4 million more than what was expected from demographic trends alone. For many, returning to a crowded work environment has not seemed appealing. For others, the isolation of working alone was a reason to leave, because many worked mostly for the relationships and enjoyment of contact with colleagues.

Among this population, nearly 1 million delayed returning to work because of a long pandemic and a recovery that took a year or more before they could return.

The Great Reimagination: Four Shifts You Need to Be Aware of

Although the Great Resignation has been a huge challenge to CEOs, there could be an upside. Many companies are finding a way to protect themselves from an even bigger shift later. But withstanding further shocks this requires a basic change in workplace systems. Every company needs to recruit and retain workers. But there are four future key shifts that will have an impact.

SHIFT NUMBER ONE: HIRING FOR SKILLS INSTEAD OF JOBS

Instead of hiring to a job, you should be thinking about the required skills for getting a job done. Instead of relying on academic degrees and previous job-specific experience, employers can train both current employees and new hires to succeed in new roles. Because of this, many companies are searching for generalists instead of specialists. In a tight job market, it may be easier to retrain current employees or hire generalists with the intent of training, even in the beginning stages of employment.

SHIFT NUMBER TWO:
HIRING FOR PROJECTS INSTEAD OF EMPLOYEES

Often a company has employees who possess certain job skills. When new projects are needed, it is sometimes difficult and slow to train employees up. It could be easier to hire contractors, gig workers, and other ad hoc workers to get results. When pharmaceutical giant AstraZeneca was tasked with creating a Covid-19 vaccine, they created tiger teams according to the project's requirements. (A tiger team is a group of cross-functional experts brought together to solve a specific problem or critical issue.) They also partnered with academia and regulatory authorities to streamline the process.

Many companies encourage pay audits for highly valued workers to make sure that wages are competitive and the workers are compensated fairly when a competitor approaches them to recruit. While money is rarely the reason people leave, it is demotivating to knowing that a competitor will pay substantially more for a position. The big three airlines, American, United, and Delta are all in a constant competitive battle to compensate their workers. The problem is that union contracts often last many years. When one airline contract is negotiated, the other two airlines' workers discover they are paid less than their competitors. Because of seniority, this is rarely a cause for moving employment, but it is demotivating for the workers.

To source any new hires, many companies should keep in contact with workers who have taken career breaks, like caregivers and those on leave. They could even contact those with physical disabilities, as well as the long-term unemployed, to fill in the gaps. The Israeli defense forces employ individuals with autism to inspect photographs of tunnels between Israel and Gaza for breaches—a job that may not be suitable for many who are not on the autism spectrum. SAP, a German company, has shown a 90 percent retention rate since they started their autism worker program in 2013.

SHIFT NUMBER THREE: FROM PART-TIME TO FLEX EVERYTHING

Many companies are now looking at workers less to benefit the company than to create value for employees, whom they regard as key stakeholders. These companies realize that they will be more successful and profitable by treating employees as whole human beings rather than mere workers. Doug Parker, former CEO with American Airlines, once stated that if employees are treated well, they will in turn treat customers well.

When one company created a program giving the workers a choice on how and where they want to work, productivity increased. If the remote work environment mandated by Covid-19 was any lesson, managers learned to focus on outcomes instead of in-office face time.

SHIFT NUMBER FOUR:
MAKE CONSTANT SMALL ADJUSTMENTS

Many companies try to predict economic and market trends up to five years in the future. But successful change rarely occurs in giant leaps. It is much more easily accomplished in small steps. As boxer Mike Tyson once said, "Every boxer has a plan until they get hit in the face." Successful companies encourage a culture of experimentation, ongoing learning, and risk-taking.

A organization focused on learning analyzes and builds on past failures and successes. It also develops a culture of lifelong learning and encourages workers to constantly build their skills.

During the Great Resignation, many workers over fifty-five retired because of boredom, lack of accomplishment, and disengagement. They had put their time in but couldn't find a reason to stay in their job. Some workers enjoyed colleague relationships and missed the camaraderie and engagement after they left. Many of these workers rejoined companies who engaged them in learning environments, skill building, and interesting projects. They were not always motivated by money; it was also because of the sense of accomplishment, stimulation, and relationships that the job offered.

Consequently, managers have an opportunity to contact past workers and offer them interesting projects, training, and reimagined job roles. Many of those who left during the Great Resignation can be enticed to rejoin their companies.

Throughout this book, we will discuss these four shifts. We will dig deeper into sourcing workers, finding out what will entice them to stay, and developing creative ways to retain the most valuable people.

RECRUITING MISTAKES

As the economy improves, companies are expanding and hiring. Unfortunately, most companies, including the most sophisticated, will have trouble getting good people. A big reason for this difficulty is waiting to look for a candidate until there is a job opening. Instead of a constant candidate quest, the only time most managers recruit is when they become desperate.

I recently spoke to a trucking group in St. George, Utah. After interviewing three business owners in preparation for my speech, I realized that hiring truckers was not their only issue. At the time the Utah unemployment rate was 3.2 percent. They had trouble getting administrative workers, let alone drivers. Most managers thought only of paying more money than the nearest competitor. But this creates a cycle in which drivers move from job to job every six months for higher pay. Some owners have become savvy about this strategy, which resembles credit card promotions. They are now paying retention as well as signing bonuses. The retention fee, often 25 percent of an annual salary, is paid after one year.

You will learn later in this book that money is very attractive to new candidates, but it is a poor retention tool. Your company may have great health insurance, wonderful employee engagement initiatives, and even room for advancement. But try telling that to a new candidate. They've heard it all before. They consider most promises to be just noise. This is why it's so important to listen to candidates in the beginning. If you can find out their goals and objectives, then focus your company's benefits on what the candidate wants, your recruiting will be much more successful.

You will also learn that great recruiters require great sales skills, while retention and training require great listening skills. The better your people skills overall, the more effective you will be at recruiting, hiring, and retaining great people.

You are about to learn three huge benefits in this book:

1. How to find great people.
2. Five secrets to use in interviewing candidates.
3. Since the best way to hire is to retain, you will learn the main reasons people leave and how to retain them longer.

According to the National Federation of Independent Businesses, 67 percent of business owners and managers say hiring good people is their biggest problem. In the same study, 80 percent said hiring the right people will determine whether their business will succeed.

I speak a lot in the financial services business. Managers in the life insurance industry recruit constantly. They judge success as retaining 15 percent of new hires after four years. And you think you have a hard time of finding and keeping great people?

MANY QUIT BEFORE SIX MONTHS

Recent research has shown there is a 31 percent chance that those you hire will quit within six months. This often happens because the candidate is sold instead of listened to. The candidate is often evaluated based on the manager's desperation to hire instead of systematic interviewing techniques. Think of it this way: if you hire someone who quits within one year for any reason, it's not their problem. It's your mistake for selecting the wrong person.

During a semipro baseball game, a bench warmer asked the manager if he could be put in the batting lineup. The manager said, "You're an OK outfielder, but you are also the worst hitter on the team. You will just strike out, and the fans will boo." The player said, "We are getting beat 5–0 in the eighth inning. What have you got to lose?" The manager put him in the lineup as a designated hitter. The pitcher stood at the mound, looked at the catcher for a signal and threw a fast ball. Strike one. This time the pitcher put his index finger on top of the ball and threw a slider: strike two. A slower lazy ball was thrown outside for ball one. But this time the pitcher bore down and threw a 96-mph curve for strike three. The batter was out. The crowd started to boo. The batter walked back to the dugout. The manager said, "Can you hear the boos? The fans hate you." The player said, "No, sir. They are booing you for putting me in."

It's not that the candidate has a problem for quitting too early; it's that you didn't follow a systematic "best practices" approach. The most egregious mistake is to make a bad hire. This means that you not only picked the wrong person but also failed to check with previous employers about past behavior.

It's like the old story about the scorpion and the frog. The scorpion wanted to cross a pond and asked the frog for a ferry ride. The frog said no, because the scorpion would sting him. The scorpion said that was crazy, since they would both drown. The frog reluctantly allowed the scorpion on his back and started his swim. Halfway across, the scorpion lined up his stinger over the frog's head and struck. The frog asked, "Why? Now we'll both die." The scorpion said, "I can't change my nature."

People really don't change. The way a candidate has behaved in the past indicates how they will act in the future. Your job is to discover past behavior.

The worst outcome? You hire a candidate who quits or gets fired within the first year. This mistake costs an average of eight months of salary in searching and training a new person. Good leaders make mistakes. Great leaders learn from hiring mistakes and don't make the same ones in the future.

1

Why Finding Great People is Critical

A few years ago, Staples office supply ran a TV commercial showing a worker labeling prices on shelf products. Nearly done, his manager walked up and said, "We are lowering prices. Go and do it again." The worker said, "Great! I can't wait to lower prices. I love this job!" I bet you have never seen a worker like that in your business.

I have a shocker. If you hire someone under thirty-five years of age, there is a high likelihood they will stay with you 2.6 years. In the 1980s, Ronald Reagan was faced with a 12 percent unemployment rate. In President Joe Biden's economy of 2021, unemployment rates ranged from 3.9 percent to slightly over 5 percent, depending on the state, but the labor participation rate was among the lowest since 2012, as folks became part of the Great Resignation. More and more left because of burnout. In 2022, *The Wall Street Journal* reported that paralegal workers in law firms left at such a clip that they were demanding as much as associate attorney salaries. Many made $300,000 and more to stay and even join a firm.

During Jimmy Carter's administration, a bad economy, combined with 18 percent interest rates, left many people out of work. Ronald Reagan's critics said he could never get unemployment below 5 percent—on the grounds that 5 percent of the workforce is unemployable: They don't want to work. They won't show up. They are lazy. They can't hold a job. I said this during a speech to a broadcasting group, joking that the unemployment rate now is 4 percent. That means 1 percent of your employees don't even want to work for you. They laughed knowingly, but it is true. We will always have a certain percentage of individuals who are unemployable, but 5 percent seems close to full employment in America. When everybody who wants to work has a job, you'd better get really good at recruiting.

With all the government handouts workers can get, 5 percent is an especially important statistic. According to one Philadelphia NBC TV broadcast, a family of four can receive more than $85,000 per year by signing up for all the benefits available to them without working a single day. A recent presidential candidate said that income inequality is so bad that the top 1 percent make sixty times more than those below the poverty line. But if you consider the tax burden on that top 1 percent and the government transfers available to those below the poverty line, inequality narrows to eight times instead of sixty.

All of this makes it very difficult to find people who actually want to work. One of my clients can't find a sales rep because the unemployed can get jobless benefits for years. Those benefits pay only slightly below what my client can offer.

As any economy enters a slowdown or recession, unemployment rates will increase. In response to inflation, the Federal Reserve increases interest rates, causing employers to fear a slowdown in sales and revenues. Businesses postpone or freeze hiring plans. But as long as unemployment is below 7–8 percent, finding good people will always be a challenge. The two missions of the Federal Reserve are low unemployment and low inflation. In a way, the Federal Reserve's success will make your task of hiring good people challenging. Hiring is always a moving target. At times, you can't find good people because there aren't enough who are qualified. At other times, candidates are more plentiful. But you always need to be able to select and retain great people.

Provide Good Training to Unskilled Workers?

Is finding great people really all that important? Can't you just hire anyone and train them for the job? I constantly hear about managers' desperation to fill seats. This often happens with recent college graduates. Managers blindly hire experience without evaluating whether the candidate will be successful at the new company.

Many years ago, when I was speaking in Chicago, George Raveling, the legendary basketball coach, was in my audience. At the time he was newly hired at USC. While I was signing books, he asked if I would speak to his coaching staff. I said, "Great, coach. I would love to, but how many will attend?" I was thinking his coaches plus all the players and boosters would be an audience of hundreds. This is what I am used to.

He said, "Only five."

"Only five? Wow. Coach, you want me to speak to five people?"

"Yep, just our coaches."

"What do you want me to speak on?"

"People skills, relationship skills, sales skills, just like I heard you speak on today."

A few weeks later, I arrived at the USC field house for my presentation. I was an hour early. All six of the coaches were already in the meeting room, staring at me while I set up. I said, "Coach, am I late?" Raveling said, "No, we are all set to listen." To have your audience stare at you for thirty minutes while you set up for your speech is very intimidating. During the presentation, I spoke about listening skills, persuasion techniques, and even referral generation techniques. I spoke about advanced neurolinguistic (NLP) communication skills and even how to spot when people are lying and telling the truth. (I'll explain this later.) The coaches voraciously took notes.

After the three-hour speech, coach Raveling took me out to lunch. He said the coaches loved my presentation. He said, "Ten percent of what we do is coaching. Ninety percent of our job is recruiting. The players bring their shoes to USC. We just shine them up!" An amazing lesson from a coach whose career was made based on his recruiting and selection ability.

Recruiting the Right People

One problem in recruiting is the sheer volume of people you have to interview. Even when you use job boards like Zip Recruiter, Indeed, and LinkedIn, you will spend days reading résumés and talking to candidates. Don't be fooled by the ads. You won't be able to read a résumé, attend an interview, and hire a great person. If that were true, dating websites like Match.com would only set up perfect dates. You would meet your soul mate on the first date.

Job boards say they will match up the skills you need to the candidate. They also promise to search out the candidates best suited for your needs. But you still have to make sure the candidate will be successful at your company. You have to interview and talk to the recruit.

Often job boards or external recruiters will cost hundreds or thousands of dollars. Wouldn't you rather save the money and source your own candidates? Wouldn't it benefit you to do all this with a minimum of wasted hours?

Filtering Good Candidates from the Crazies

I jokingly tell audiences that if they don't screen candidates, they will go crazy. Not only is it a total waste of time, but the manager will talk to a plethora of neurotic, if not psychotic, people. I've interviewed candidates who spent the whole time talking about bad marriages. If that is not OK on a blind date, why would they think it's OK in an interview?

I have also interviewed candidates who complained about their previous jobs. They failed to understand that I was searching for someone for a new job instead of litigating the issues of the last one. It's almost like going on a blind date. You can surmise within ten minutes if the person is compatible. But sometimes you feel compelled to stick it out for the next hour, not wanting to be rude by ending the encounter.

One TV commercial explored what would happen if first dates were totally blunt. It showed a couple on a blind date at dinner. The woman said, "If you call, I will not pick up the phone." The man said, "I hope you're not expecting a phone call." The woman said, "How quickly can I leave?" The man said, "I wonder if can get away with paying half the bill." This was comical because it was so real.

One of my graduate school psych professors jokingly told us the difference between neurotics and psychotics. A neurotic will build sandcastles in the sky. A psychotic will move into them. And the psychologist will collect the rent.

My favorite dichotomy between neurotics and psychotics has to do with a math question. How much is two plus two? A psychotic, who has no sense of reality, will say, "Sixteen, thirty-two, five, two hundred." A neurotic will answer, "Four," but will then add, "I hate it when it's four all the time. Why can't it be five once in a while?"

Most managers post an ad in a newspaper or online job board and get fifty or sixty responses. Most of the responses won't measure up. Many candidates aren't really qualified for the job but want to hear all about your opening.

At best, you will spend about fifteen minutes on the phone with each candidate, totally wasting your time. Or you could let one of your staff screen them. If your staff has little training, they may be turning away good candidates and booking interviews with bad ones.

Virtual Voice Mail

There is a great way to evaluate people in seconds without wasting your valuable time. It's called *virtual voice mail*. It's a way to listen to voice mails from candidates to evaluate whether or not they are qualified. First, get a voice mail line that no one will answer. This can be a back line in your company. You can even call your phone provider and get a dedicated voice mail line for about $25. If you have a VoIP (voice over Internet protocol) service, it's called a *soft phone*. Next, put a very short ad on an online job board like Indeed, Craigslist, Zip Recruiter, a college job board, or any other ad vehicle you think will get a good response. In the ad, you need to leave a short message like:

> *Sales rep needed for successful (your industry) company. High income and great training. Five years' experience and (type of experience you need) required. For more information call (voice mail phone number).*

Using your area code instead of an 800 number will let them know you are local. If you use a toll-free number, you will get fewer calls.

You need to leave a detailed voice mail announcement to explain what your business is, what you produce, what the job entails, the hours, and any benefits. You need to be thorough. But also realize you are trying to attract candidates, not scare them away. At the end of the message, use this closing phrase: "Please leave up to a one-minute message on what experience you have that has prepared you to be successful at this position. Please also leave your name, phone number, and e-mail contact information." That's it.

As you listen to the message, pay attention to their energy and past performance. This is the first filter in finding good people. You need to listen to whether they answered the question. You will hear some candidates say, "Yes, I am interested in the job. Here is my phone number." But the response you want is, "My name is John. I worked at a similar company as yours and increased sales by 35 percent over the last year. I would like to hear more about your company and see if it is a good fit."

Listen as if you were buying from this person. If they don't have enough energy, they won't sound good to your customers and your staff. But most importantly, did they tell you what they did that has prepared them for the job? Did they answer the question? If they didn't, they may not listen well after you hire them.

Through this approach, you can listen and filter voice mail responses on your cell phone. You will never again waste an hour of your time in a face-to-face interview. You can call the top candidates for a follow-up appointment.

Another tip is to run your ad Thursday through Sunday for a few weeks until you get a sizable number of responses. Also put the same ad in industry magazines or newsletters. You will cut down your candidate search time by 80 percent with this technique. And you won't make yourself nuts interviewing crazy people.

Online Recruiting: The New Job Boards

One of the problems using an online recruiting company is accuracy. It's one thing to input your need for an applicant. It's quite another to find the right person.

Online services like the Zip Recruiter, LinkedIn, or Indeed will supply candidates who match their résumés to your search criteria. But it's up to you to interview the right person. You still need to ask the right questions, talk to past employers, and qualify them. The job of picking people is based on your interview skill set. Online services only bring people to you. Most recruiters think the hardest part of selection is sourcing. Actually, the most challenging part is selection and retention. If all you want to do is save time and don't care about who you hire or how long they stay, online job boards are fine. But if you are trying to get the best people and think recruiting good people is an ongoing process instead of an activity you engage in once in a while, then learning and applying your own sourcing is best. Online job board candidates are often the worst candidates available.

One of my clients used Indeed for an administrative assistant search. He received five candidate résumés. One was thirty miles away, two wanted 30 percent more money than he was willing to pay, and another had absolutely no qualifications in his industry. Online advertising cost several hundred dollars. It was a waste of time. But my client did learn to recruit consistently instead of just when he was desperate.

A Job Post That Gets Results

What is your strategy for posting on a job board? Are you trying to get as many candidates to respond as possible? Are you trying to qualify candidates before they respond?

The answer should be both. Wherever you post, you need to attract qualified candidates. But you also need to minimize time engaging with those who are not right for your search.

In a tight job market, many companies are struggling to write job descriptions that both attract and discourage. They are writing descriptions using gender-neutral language. They are trying to let the candidate know the day-to-day duties of the position. They are explaining the downsides of a job as well as communicating the strengths.

The best job descriptions also include jargon required for each position. For example, "A qualified candidate will have a command of Excel, Sales Logic, and PowerPoint graphic design." For a tax job, the description may include specific software tools that are required.

Successful job descriptions first talk about the mission and commitment of the company as well as its values. The first two paragraphs will also include how important the position is to the growth of the company in general. It will sell the company strengths as a market leader as well as job benefits. This will include a salary range and medical and retirement benefits, as well as vacation and travel policy.

Surprisingly, some of the most successful new descriptions now include day-to-day duties describing what the job actually is. For example, a marketing manager's day might include:

1. Answering about fifty emails per day.
2. Two half-hour meetings per day updating both team members and director-level management.
3. Five video-based thirty-minute conference calls per day with prospects and customers.
4. Two to three days of travel per week visiting prospects and customers.
5. Supervising website and social media staff for one to two hours per day.
6. Maintaining budget reports for about sixty minutes per week.

Not only will a successful job description inform the candidate of what a typical day looks like, it will also give the applicant an idea of what is expected of them to be successful at the position. Managers who are using the "day in the life" approach are discovering much more candidate engagement than those using a shorter description. Many are saying that jobs are filled in half the time because the applicant feels much more informed and interested.

In one California tech company, a salary range of $145,000–$175,000 was given. Directly below the salary range, a list of specific projects was listed that the team recently tackled. It discussed time frames, expectations, and final results.

Using jargon for technical positions helps filter candidates. But just as importantly, using gender-neutral pronouns will attract female candidates more effectively. Using *they* and *you* is much more effective than using *he* or *she*.

Millennial and Generation X candidates are also much more interested in how the position contributes to a company than were previous generations. They are looking for significance and impact in the positions they are applying for. For example, "sales manager" may be described as not only supervising ten regional sales professionals but helping those ten producers get to the next level of their careers and increase their incomes.

New successful job descriptions not only try to motivate the candidate to respond, but also to qualify the applicant and let them know the importance of the position and how it affects the whole team. Job descriptions that were a few paragraphs ten years ago are now two to three pages. New job descriptions have an abstract at the top of the page discussing the job and benefits. But then discuss the importance of the position, the day-to-day operations, and expectations. It is counterintuitive to think that a longer job description will turn off applicants. A three-page description is better and has much more impact than a one-pager.

The Website Is Your Brand:
The First Interview

You've made contact with a candidate. What's next? Whether they responded to an online lead or you initiated a referral, candidates will always say, "What is your website? I want to check out your company." Back in the old days, respondents would ask to be sent something. This was either a blow-off or a request to learn more.

Today candidates will vet you and your company before they talk. Half of candidates will look at your website or social media site before they interview.

Your website needs to sell your brand. Your brand must sell the opportunities you offer. It needs to appeal to both internal and external customers. Jack Welch, the legendary CEO of General Electric, once said, "We take care of our stakeholders first, then our employees. If we take care of our employees, they will take care of our customers." The former president of American Airlines, Doug Parker, says the same. During every company meeting, broadcast systemwide, he made a point of mentioning that when American Airlines takes care of their team members, they will take care of customers.

But your claims must be backed up by experience. My wife is a flight attendant for American Airlines, which seems to be constantly at odds with union employees. In the summer of 2019, the mechanics were in contract negotiations with management. The mechanics are in charge of the equipment—getting planes ready for early morning takeoff. Most airlines service and maintain their planes at night. The union slowed down the overnight process, causing many planes to be unavailable. American Airlines normally had sixty planes in reserve each day, but that year, the reserve fleet decreased to only four. This caused 5 to 10 percent of all flights to be canceled on any one day.

I was part of the mass cancellation malady. When a frequent flyer normally calls American Airlines to rebook, the top tier desk will help without comment. But that year, they would often say, "Yes, we are tired of this happening too. There is nothing we can do." It's kind of like saying, "Our airline sucks. But it's the job I have right now, so I have to be here."

This doesn't sound like a company that takes great care of its employees. Companies who take care of employees also take care of customers. I fly American Airlines because my wife works for them—that is, for no other reason than that we can fly together.

What does your website say about your brand? What does your website say about your employees and your commitment to them? Your candidate will notice whether your company is only in business to make money or has a vision to make money by putting employees first. When you put employees first, they will then put customers first. They will see whether your website mentions your great staff. They will see whether you feature employee bios and whether your staff looks happy in those photos. They will even notice your staff longevity and retention.

Hiring is a lot more than picking the right person. It is also about marketing and positioning. If your website broadcasts a commitment to supporting your staff, yet you have high turnover, the talk doesn't match the walk. There is the odd candidate who hasn't done their due diligence and just wants a job, but your goal should be to hire great people and retain them. Once they discover your company isn't what was represented, they will leave.

The Mission: How Do You Communicate Value?

On your website describe your commitment to employees. Most of the sites I have seen state, "We value our employees!" How far would you get if you said, "I value my spouse!" and stop there? You don't have to tell the world how much you love your employees. But do more than make a trite statement.

At an awards function recently, I told the audience, "My wife is very special!" Afterward, she looked at me and said, "Is that all you had to say about our thirty years of marriage? There were two hundred people in the room, and all you had to say was, I am special?" Lesson learned.

Some of the better sites I have seen report, "Our employees are so loyal that they stay with us on average fifteen years." Websites often communicate a commitment to clients. One states, "Our commitment to clients is a long-term relationship in which we communicate every three months about their goals and needs." I have also seen, "Our great staff care so much about our clients that the three-month client contact call is the first thing we organize every morning."

Another site said, "We have the sharpest and most committed staff in the industry. They always put our clients first. On every phone call or meeting, you will see their professionalism, expertise, and commitment to meeting your needs!"

These websites broadcast that they have the best people. Because of that, you will be treated better than any of their competitors.

Building a Social Media Presence That Attracts Talented People

One of the most important points in this book is that you should always be recruiting. This doesn't mean you have to make cold calls every day. It also doesn't mean that you have to spend your day interviewing for vacancies you don't yet have. But it does mean that you have to always be marketing and advertising for new candidates.

Facebook, LinkedIn, and Twitter have billions of users who post and interact on a daily basis. If you do not have a business Facebook page in addition to a company site, you are missing a great source of new talent. With LinkedIn, you can get away with a business-only page, since the site is seen as a business-to-business network. But those on LinkedIn also have a presence on Facebook and Twitter.

You should be posting on these sites at least three times every week. These posts can be anything from new information about your products and services to company initiatives and goals. The most important thing to keep in mind is to make your posts valuable to the reader. I actively participate in all three of these social media platforms. When someone posts about a skill or a business epiphany learned from mistakes or successes, I pay attention. Those who post product pitches or self-serving advertisements are often the ones I block permanently.

One of my clients is a life insurance distributor. He could talk about how good their single premium life products are, or about how much better their annuities are than the competition's. Instead his posts are often focused on techniques to better communicate with clients. Or he posts new research from retirement think tanks on what seniors want. He posts new information on retirement challenges, both monetary and psychological.

In one post, he mentioned the five biggest concerns retirees have:

1. A fear of running out of money.
2. Stock market volatility.
3. High taxes during retirement.
4. Inflation rising during retirement.
5. The cost of catastrophic illness and long-term care.

These kinds of posts have two benefits. First, they are informative to both job candidates and clients. Second, they are current and keep his company at the top of the mind to anyone curious enough to want more information.

"When you only have a hammer, you treat everything like a nail." Often companies are so wrapped with what they sell that they forget whom they sell it to and those who sell it. Every company has a product or service, but very successful leaders realize it is only a small part of their enterprise. Most companies make money from strategic vision and execution, but the execution is always about people skills and communication. Your leadership is not based on what you sell. It is based on how and what you communicate.

I recently went on an appointment with one of my coaching clients. I wanted to observe how he communicated and ran a presentation. At the prospect's house, he started the appointment chatting about their backyard and how long they lived in the neighborhood. Then he launched into the presentation. He started talking at 5:05 p.m. and ended at 6:10 p.m. When he took a breath, he looked at the couple and said, "Do you like this approach?" The couple both looked at each other, seeming surprised, and said, "We will think about it." The salesperson said, "What do you want to think about?" The couple made a trite excuse about always wanting to sleep on big decisions. The salesperson made several calls over the next few days, but the couple never responded.

This is a very good example of a product being pitched and sold. But sales are made by listening and matching needs to benefits. Communication and emotional intelligence are everything. If the salesperson could have engaged and listened, he would have had a much better chance of making the sale and helping the client.

Recruiting is the same. The better you can communicate your vision and listen to needs, the more you will attract good candidates. The more that you can communicate how much you care about your people and whom they sell to, the more you will attract great people.

In many ways, recruiting is really another form of sales. Sales is about listening and matching solutions to needs. The more you can do that, the more you will attract candidates.

How to Build a Compelling Brand

Every company around the world wants a brand that is remembered. A brand aids in communicating a mission and values. Sometimes a brand connotes great customer service and an experience better than those of other airlines, like the old United Airlines tagline: "Fly the Friendly Skies." With the current antagonism between passengers and airlines like United, that brand is no longer believable.

On one flight, an attendant purposely spilled beer on me in revenge. She had asked me to check my garment bag. There was room in the airplane closet, so I put it there. She took it off the airplane without asking and then scolded me for it. I later found out that taking a bag off without the customer's consent is against company rules. But at that moment, she was the brand. Her behavior was not congruent with a brand selling a great customer experience. The brand became meaningless.

Just saying you are the best or cheapest isn't a brand. It has to be specific to customer needs. Every one of my audio or video products states a benefit—in a sense, a brand. My Peak Performance audio tagline is "How to increase your business by 80 percent in 8 weeks!" There is no doubt about what the promise is and what the customer will get.

In an environment of intense competition for great people, you need a brand that resonates. The best candidates don't just want to be compensated fairly; they want to work for a company with a compelling brand. What is yours?

If you really want to attract great people and make recruiting a lot easier, you have to build a tangible brand. You can always fill a job opening without a clear brand. But you can't keep good people without belief in your brand.

Let's talk about the power of a brand.

1. Branding eliminates the need for mass marketing. Branding targets your market, making you an expert to those who discover you.

2. Branding differentiates you from all other competitors. When most vendors look, act and talk the same, they only compete on price. Legendary rocker Jerry Garcia once said, "You don't have to be seen as the best out there; you have to be seen as the only one out there."

3. Branding creates a reason for customers to pay you more. Branding builds confidence in the mind of your prospects that you can deliver on your promises. When they have confidence, they are unlikely to quibble over your fees. Few people would quibble with Tony Robbins over his speaking fee on a motivational subject.

4. Branding builds client loyalty. If your client knows what you are an expert at, they will not replace you with someone who is cheaper.

5. Branding also builds referrals. If you try to be everything to everybody, you will be unique to nobody. But if you define your brand, you will gain referrals from those who know what you stand for.

6. Differentiation in branding applies to everything you do: your office, your letterhead, the way your staff answers calls. Is it different? Is it better? Victoria's Secret put photos of lingerie-clad women on their billing statements.

Branding is the process of persuading your customer there is nothing in the market quite like your product or service. Evian water (*naive* spelled backwards) is such a powerful brand that the 1.5-liter size sells for more than $4—20 percent more than Budweiser, 40 percent more than Borden's milk, and over three times more than Coke.

Are you surprised to read about branding in a book on hiring? Don't forget: you are trying to attract great people. The people you want to employ need to be the best at what they do. If they don't see you and your company as an opportunity, they will take a look at another company that is more attractive.

Another area that your brand needs to be distinctive in is price. If your company has a brand that's differentiated, candidates will see opportunities instead of just a paycheck. If they can see future growth, upward mobility, and a career future, they may not consider salary as so important. A paycheck always needs to be competitive with what they could make elsewhere. But as you will read further in this book, money is not what retains great people. In fact, money is almost always the last reason why good people leave.

But first, what is your brand? What makes it unique? What does it do that stands out? What is your personal brand? If you tell somebody at a cocktail party what you do, do they respond with, "Wow, I would like to hear more about that!" Or do they say, "That's nice" and reach for a canapé?

A brand is . . .
- An outward expression of a company.
- The difference between you and your competitors.
- The reason employees and clients choose you and not a cheaper version.
- The trust that is generated between you and your clients and employees.
- What your clients and customers say you are, not what you think you are.

A brand is not . . .
- A logo.
- A product.
- A price. Discounters never survive. There are always competitors trying to beat your price. But a solid brand that also offers competitive pricing will survive.

Consider these questions in creating your own brand.
1. How do your employees describe your company?
2. How do your clients describe your company?
3. What do your clients value most about what you and your company do for them?
4. What makes you and your company unique?
5. What are the intangible benefits your employees value most?
6. What are the intangible benefits your clients value most?
7. Why do your employees continue working for you and your company?
8. Why do your clients stay? Have you ever asked them this question?

It's likely that you've never asked your clients and employees even a few of these. You'll be surprised. Often when I ask my coaching clients why their own clients stay, I hear about advanced financial planning ability, or their technology and how good they are at placing mortgages. I even hear how effective they are at getting competitive pricing.

Then I ask my clients to present the same questions to their own clients. The answers are never about technology, pricing, or technical ability. They are always about the ability to listen, frequency of contact, and responsiveness to concerns.

The same is true of your own employees. You probably think they stay because of a paycheck or how much they love the job. You may even think they feel lucky to be working for you. The truth is, the job benefits they value most are surprising. They probably value your mentorship, training, and upward mobility. I'm sure they value work relationships.

Take some time over the next week and ask each of your team members: What do you value most in working here? What keeps you in this job? You may not want to hear the answers. You may also be too busy to effect any changes indicated by these conversations. But if you don't know why people stay with you or why they leave, you will never recruit and retain a great team over the long term.

Selecting Experience?

Here's another question. Is hiring for experience generally a good bet? This is tricky, because the person you recruit from a competitor may be bringing their same problems to your company. Ten years ago, one of my mortgage company clients lost a mediocre salesperson. They were glad to get rid of him but shocked by whom he went to. He was recruited by one of the biggest mortgage origination companies in the US. I was surprised that they didn't investigate whether he was successful with his prior company.

There is another reason why experience may not benefit you, and that is culture. No two companies have the same culture. A candidate may have been successful with one company yet may be unsuccessful with yours.

In 1999, the Houston Rockets had some of the best pro basketball players on the face of the earth. They had Scottie Pippen and Hakeem Olajuwon, two of the highest-paid stars of the day. But the Rockets were close to last place that year in the NBA standings. The reason: Pippen and Olajuwon couldn't play together. They were not a team.

One way to select for teamwork with your candidates is to look at their past employment. Do they have a history of moving from firm to firm? Did you find out whether they had conflicts with past employers? It will become quickly apparent whether they will also have problems with your company.

In 1988, I lost another salesperson and was busy interviewing candidates to fill the position. I normally don't recommend headhunters, but I was in a bind to find somebody quickly. The headhunter I spoke to was Andrea. After I described the job, she asked to interview for it. She didn't know anything about my industry. She knew even less about our sales systems. But the communication skill set she learned in the recruitment business turned out to be the same that made her successful booking me as a speaker.

Hotelier Bill Marriott was once asked, "How do you train people to be so friendly?" He answered, "I don't. I hire friendly people."

2

Where to Look

here do you go for great people? What are the best areas to recruit from? Here are some places. I'm sure you can think of others, but here are a few to start.

Passive versus Active Candidates

Recruiting is tough. Not only do you have to source great people, you have to make sure they are right for the job. Some candidates are easy to find. Others are tough. The ones who are actively looking don't require as much pursuing as those who aren't.

The candidates currently looking to change jobs are called *active candidates.* The ones not looking but still interested in other opportunities are called *passive candidates.* You will read several times in this book that 69 percent of those currently employed are active candidates. These are the ones likely to respond to any sort of outreach for a new opportunity.

You will also find that an additional 14 percent of the job force aren't actively looking but would consider a new opportunity. These folks are passive candidates. They aren't unhappy enough to leave but can be persuaded. They aren't as responsive to outreach or job posts. They have to be proactively contacted and consistently pursued.

Some of the candidate sourcing strategies below will help you contact active job seekers. Later, we will discuss ways to source passive candidates.

Here are five basic areas for finding good people.

MEDIA ADS

Newspaper and magazine ads are not as popular now as online media. Some local weekly newspapers can be good. Craigslist can be effective for administrative people. Indeed.com and ZipRecruiter.com are good for higher-level candidates. But if you use the virtual voice mail method for attracting candidates that I mentioned in the previous chapter, any media source can be good for pulling people in without wasting a lot of time. I personally have used Craigslist for administrative positions, and when the unemployment rate is higher than 5 percent, have received more than sixty responses from every ad. With low unemployment, those response rates will certainly be lower as well. The problem is generally not getting candidates to respond; it's always looking for the good ones, challenges like the Great Resignation notwithstanding.

TEMP AGENCIES AND SEARCH FIRMS

Unless you are looking for a midlevel manager, a temp company will allow you to evaluate someone while actually doing the job. Most temp companies charge a 35 percent premium, but that is cheap compared to a bad hire. I like the idea of someone working on a trial basis at first.

One of my coaching clients told a candidate they were on probation for three months. I said, "Were they recently convicted?" Doesn't three months' probation sound as if they were just released from prison? You are not only trying to select the right person, you also need to retain them. What I usually say is that we will "evaluate" each other over the next few months and see if this is the right fit. Most candidates are happy with that agreement, since they don't want a bad experience either.

One trucking company client uses temp agencies exclusively. It saves a lot of time, mostly in selecting administrative staff. Temp agencies have already done some legwork: they won't send over flaky people. Nor will they risk introducing you to somebody who can't do the job. This provides you with a minimum level of ability, which helps if you don't have the time to recruit.

Nevertheless, there are several problems with using temp agencies as your recruiting source. First is the cost. You will pay one-third more to recruit through a temp agency. If you hire the temp within three to six months, you will pay a surcharge for the first year. This can become very expensive.

Search firms live on saving you time. If you don't have good recruiting systems and don't have the time to search for good people, engaging them may be your answer. But they also will charge up to 100 percent of the candidate's first year's salary. They may also give you a time guarantee, but that doesn't mean you will hire somebody good. It only gives you some insurance that the employee will stay the whole year.

In 1986, I hired a woman through a search firm to market me as a speaker. She lasted one year and two weeks, then quit. I was thirty-one years old and didn't know the difference. She had made a deal with the search firm that her tenure would be at least one year—to get past any guarantee commitment I made with the recruiter. I never made that mistake again.

JOB FAIRS

They are a great way to meet new candidates. It's a way to talk about your brand and collect a mailing list. Most of the companies that exhibit at job fairs are looking to build a contact list. Job fairs are not the best places to fill a vacancy, but they are great places to build a future team. Often you will see job fairs at college campuses, possibly even at county fairs. Most importantly, job fairs are places to engage with passive candidates.

Just in case you don't want to spend a weekend at a booth, a virtual job fair may be the answer. In reality, this is simply a webinar with a question-and-answer segment. It could be one hour per week for four weeks. It could even be once every quarter. The important thing is to attend these events consistently. A virtual job fair could be a well-advertised conference call allowing a few hundred attendees.

An effective virtual job fair will consist of a panel describing various job positions. They could be one person representing product and development, administration, finance, and even sales. An effective way is to allow each to describe their position for five minutes and then answer questions for another ten minutes.

Whether you spend the weekend at an in-person job fair or in a virtual fair, building a list of passive job seekers is the goal.

As you are beginning to learn, recruiting is more than filling a job vacancy. It's about 24/7 wall-to-wall engagement. There is not a week that goes by when I don't receive an offer for a white paper. (A white paper is a specialized report published by companies on topic of interest. White papers are usually an attempt to gain leads. White paper topic examples are strategic planning, management by objectives, speaking skills, and even time management.) Their purpose is not only to educate readers but to build a database. I don't think many are trying to recruit. Instead, they are trying to collect potential buyers. This technique is also very effective in building engagement with future job candidates.

I wrote an article, "How to Increase Closing Ratios," for a financial planning magazine a few months ago. In my bio at the end of the article, I offered to send a video to any reader who would respond with their email and phone number. I received more than sixty responses to that one article. I asked my assistant Bethany to book phone appointments with the respondents. My only goal was to find out more about them and possibly get a referral to an executive who could hire me as a speaker. The technique worked wonderfully. The readers received more information on closing techniques, and I received referrals in an effort to build my speaking business.

You could do the same with a white paper. Offer a document or video on a topic the reader is interested in. The most important thing is to make contact on the phone. Do not just correspond. It's important to find out something about the person. Develop some kind of personal relationship. Only then can you engage them for a future position. If all you do is get an email address, there is no reason for them to remember you. But if you could talk to them and find out more, you have the beginnings of developing a passive contact list that you can use as a resource when you need somebody.

The mindset of a millennial often focuses on screen time, with less emphasis on relationships. But a tech focus is not only limited to millennials. It can also attract baby boomers as well. I play tennis with a group of guys on Thursday nights. Twelve of us usually show up. After tennis, the group goes out to a late dinner and a few drinks at a local restaurant.

One week I was on a speaking trip. But I heard that one of the group, Tony, was unhappy with a server and refused to tip her. He left his share of the bill and went to the bathroom. Gabe, another of our players, felt guilty about not tipping the server and covered Tony. When Tony got back, he heard that Gabe paid his part and went ballistic. It was Gabe's money, but Tony still felt slighted. Gabe is a property and casualty insurance agent and had five of Tony's policies.

The next day, Gabe sent a phone text trying to calm his friend down. Tony shot a note back saying Gabe had no right to countermand his tipping wishes. This texting went back and forth a few times. Each exchange became more pronounced.

Finally, Tony told Gabe to cancel all his policies, and the texting stopped. When I heard the story, the solution became obvious. Why not pick up the phone and talk? Crisis could have been averted. Gabe is a good friend, so I let him have it. Email and texting are for transactions; face-to-face and phone interactions are for relationships. Was Tony a relationship or a transaction? If he was a relationship, why treat him like a transaction?

The same is true of recruiting. You would never hire someone merely on the basis of their résumé, online or on paper. Why not build better relationships with passive candidates? Making a call or even seeing them face-to-face every three months will build your human reserves. Sending an email or text will only build your CRM (customer relationship management) list.

SCHOOLS AND COLLEGES

Some of the best places to get candidates are college job boards and vocational schools. These schools are now required by the US government to prove a minimum job placement rate at graduation to get government-funded loans for their students. Many years ago, I gave a speech to Enterprise Rent-A-Car. There were 500 twenty-somethings in my audience. Forty-five years old at the time, I felt like the old man from the sea. I asked the senior VP client why the group was so young. He said Enterprise is the biggest recruiter of college graduates in America. Since they have such a great training program, they attract and retain smart graduates. One of my clients keeps an ad running on a college job board consistently every week. She gets about five phone calls from candidates and always has a fresh group to interview once she has an opening. Recruiting is not about filling a vacancy. It is about always making sure your human resource pipeline is full.

One of my coaching clients lost a key support staffer, who went to work in his parents' company. My client didn't know where to look for someone he could both afford and retain. He contacted a college dean that he knew from his seminars there. My client did seminars for a few years and thought the dean might help.

The finance dean graduated 100 students per year and knew the good from the bad. Most employers don't realize that colleges are measured not only by the quality of their education, but also by how many students find jobs after graduation. He was more than happy to suggest his best students for interviews. My client spoke to about five top-level students and picked Courtney.

College graduates are unlikely to stay more than three years in their first job. In fact, most will change careers seven times before they find one they are passionate about. My client made sure he knew what Courtney's goals were. He spoke to her every three months about career progression. His goal was to make sure her goals were always at the top of his mind. The only thing worse about losing a key person is to lose them too soon with no notice.

There are many ways you can interact with college talent sources. You can visit an outplacement office. You can also get to know the dean supervising students in an area of expertise you are looking for. The wrong thing to do is to *only* post a notice on their job board. This is better than a newspaper, but not much.

Remember, recruiting is about relationships. It is not just about advertising.

One of my coaching clients makes a yearly donation to the local college business department. It's not much, but $500 every semester goes a long way to extend a limited teaching budget. Whenever he needs a candidate or even an intern, he talks to the business school department head. The donation actually gets the business coordinator to announce the job opening in each class. How is that for recruiting?

Another of my coaching clients is now teaching at a college in Berkeley, California. I'm sure he likes to teach; I'm also sure that he wants to give back to his field. But the real reason he is spending three evenings a week teaching is to generate new candidates for his own business. In trying to recruit advisors, the pool of available good candidates is small. But his goal is to engage with up to thirty students, hoping that he can find a couple that are promising.

As my client teaches the class, he will be able to learn who the motivated students are and those who just slide along. He will also be able to see how quick they are on their feet as well as getting a good sense of their emotional intelligence. It's almost as if he were doing a four-month job interview.

I know within a few weeks whether a coaching client will succeed. It's often as simple as whether they follow up and do their homework. Sometimes I see a level of initiative that is not apparent in other clients. But one thing is for sure: the superstars always shine. They always apply the techniques we discuss and do what they say they will do. There's no magic. There is no silver bullet. They just show up and keep their promises.

It can be a wonderful idea for you to teach a college or vocational class. Not only will you develop professional skills, but you will also be able to expand your own staff by interviewing new recruits during the months of your tenure.

RECRUITING FROM WITHIN

Before you search outside, perhaps you should look inside. There are people working for you right now who could do a wonderful job if promoted to a higher position. One of my clients in New Jersey needed an office manager. Joe was all set to advertise and go through the hiring process. His receptionist, Linda, seemed energetic and diligent. I asked Joe if she had enough successful past performance and energy to be a good office manager. I asked him if she had the mindset to herd cats. He laughed and said, "I know I can't do it. Let's give her a shot."

Linda was a diamond in the rough. After five years, Joe has found someone who is not only loyal but diligent and thorough. The same skills that made her successful as a receptionist seem to make her a good office manager. As Jim Collins, author of *Good to Great*, once said, "Before you kick someone off the bus, move them to another seat."

Who can you think of right now with the ability to move up? Who in your company can you develop into someone who can make a contribution? The wonderful thing about advancing people from within is communicating to the rest that they can also move up in the organization. This will increase morale and motivation. Whenever you have a job opening, your first thought should be to move somebody up within your own company.

Thirty-five years ago, I lost an excellent marketing person. One of my competitors promised her a 35 percent increase in pay and 50 percent more in commissions. You could argue that she was not loyal. But everything else being equal, I would have made the same choice if I were in her situation.

Before the Internet, we only had print classifieds and search firms to recruit. I was looking at a lot of expense in sourcing a new marketer. My administrative assistant, Sheri, asked if I would give her a shot. I never thought about her as a salesperson. But she said her father ran a recording studio and she was in charge of booking studio time. She was always personable and had a great level of emotional intelligence. I hired her because I didn't want to go through the effort of interviewing. Sheri sold speeches for me for nearly twenty years and did an excellent job. Always look within before you spend money looking without.

Recruiting Those Who Need a Job Versus Those You Can Attract

More about active versus passive candidates: Active candidates are searching for employment. Often, they don't have a job because of a recent termination or they left the last employer. These are the folks who are the most available and sometimes the least desirable. These are also the candidates with the most experience interviewing. They often know your questions and answers before you ask them.

Since active candidates are the easiest to engage, they are also the most tempting to hire. Poor recruiters will consider them out of desperation. Possibly these managers have been searching for months without success. Their expectation of quality lowers by the day. They rationalize that getting anybody in the job is better than to keep looking. It's like one of my single female friends saying that good men are hard to find. If they can't find Mr. Right, they settle for Mr. Right Now. This may be a harmless dating strategy, but it will destroy your business. Don't hire Mr. or Ms. Right Now.

If 80 percent of what you do depends on hiring great people, you'd better learn how to recruit great people. Great people usually don't appear when you are desperate. They appear because you are consistently looking. Your net is cast constantly to find someone good. Sometimes this entails creating a job for a great person, even though you don't have a current opening. Great people are hard to find. Maybe it's better to hire them now instead of hoping you will get lucky and find someone good when the opening appears.

In 1981, I was a new PhD graduate. California was in the middle of a deep recession. I knew I didn't want to go into academia. I didn't want to get stuck in the endless cycle of teaching and research. The only opportunity was to become an assistant and then associate professor of psychology. If I was really lucky, and really good, I could reach tenure.

The other career path was clinical psychology. My wife says that I don't have an empathic gene in my body. When someone complains about a frivolous experience, my first inclination is to tell them what to do.

In one episode of the Showtime series *The Affair*, a woman who was cheated on by her unfaithful husband moved to Malibu, California. Remarried, she lived in a mansion overlooking the Pacific. Married to a surgeon, she didn't have much to do. In one scene, she was on a couch talking to a psychiatrist, complaining about the blue skies and the boredom of looking at the same sparkling blue Pacific Ocean, day after day. The therapist listened attentively and said, "Let me get this straight. You're tired of the clear blue skies and the boringly blue Pacific. That has to be difficult." I would have recapped her words followed by my opinion: "There are about 6 billion people with much more difficult lives than yours. Get out of my office, volunteer at a soup kitchen, and stop wasting my time." I would never have succeeded as a psychotherapist.

My career options were limited. Either become a professor or psychotherapist, or get a job in the real world. I picked the latter. But the only job I was offered was as a shoe store manager in San Diego. I learned about an IBM competitor named Honeywell. They didn't have an opening, but the manager of the San Diego branch was willing to talk. I prepared for the interview by learning as much as I could about this mainframe computer supplier, the competition from IBM, and even Honeywell's history. I think the manager was trying to test me after a few minutes of rapport by asking what I knew about Honeywell. I pulled out my manila folder with one inch of research and started to recite not only their sales figures for the year but also what I saw as the threat IBM presented to Honeywell over the next five years. You could see the manager sit forward in his chair with his eyebrows arched. He stood up and asked me to wait. He was gone for nearly twenty minutes. I didn't know what to do. I read all the brochures on his coffee table and just waited. Finally, he came back and said he called his divisional manager. They found an opening in Los Angeles. Was I willing to relocate, and did I want the job?

The unemployment rate in 1981 was nearly 12 percent. I had no job prospects and was thinking about going back to college for an MBA. But this branch manager created a job for me.

What would you do if you found a good candidate? You could make them wait for a vacancy. You could even keep in contact every few months. Or you can improve your ability to source good people and hire someone good now for a need in the future. What would you do?

Recruiting Passive Candidates

The second type of candidates is passive ones. According to one study reported by *Business Insider* magazine, 95 percent of workers are thinking about quitting their jobs because of burnout. Passive candidates are looking, but not very hard. Most job satisfaction studies show that 83 percent of workers don't like their jobs, and 69 percent would leave today for a better opportunity. This means that 83 percent of workers will respond if engaged. They don't have résumés on job boards like Indeed, Monster, ZipRecruiter, or Glassdoor, but that doesn't mean they wouldn't entertain possibilities. In a way, they are waiting for your phone call. They are hoping for someone to ask them if they want to go to the prom. They are waiting to be charmed and attended to. They are waiting for new opportunities. But they are not planning to quit their positions.

Corporations tend to be very good at attracting and engaging passive candidates. Small companies tend to be good at sourcing active candidates, focused on filling an immediate vacancy. As I stated before, if you hire because of a current need, you may not get right person. This is where retention suffers, but also productivity.

Your job is to keep a big reservoir of passive candidates. You can then consistently filter those willing to make a job change. Just because they're not ready to make a change now doesn't mean they won't be available in the future. The 83 percent of workers who are unhappy in their jobs might not be motivated to change jobs now, but they are always looking for new opportunities. Your job is to engage with them right now with an eye toward hiring in the future.

One of my coaching clients, Kevin, runs an independent financial marketing organization. He was looking for a marketer and couldn't find anybody good. While chatting over a cup of coffee with a waiter at his favorite restaurant, Kevin realized that the competencies needed in a marketer were also the skills displayed by the server. The only variable was consistency. Would the server make consistent phone calls and be unfazed by rejection?

While the waiter didn't have any direct sales experience, Kevin improvised. He asked the waiter how he did at parties when he didn't know anyone. He asked how the waiter coped with negative restaurant customers. He even asked if the waiter had any problems getting to work on time. Kevin hired the waiter and never looked back. The waiter turned telemarketer is engaging and coachable, and even copes well with rejection. Who would have thought that a restaurant waiter possessed the same skills and talents that made for a good insurance marketer?

Recently, one of my coaching clients said he always defers to his HR people when he needs a good candidate. He is way too busy to search when he doesn't have a need. At a recent conference speaking to HR folks, one professional said they don't have enough time to be engaging with passive candidates. They respond only when there is a vacancy, and not before.

This creates a Catch-22 situation. The small business manager doesn't have enough time to look for candidates. The HR professional doesn't have time either. If the unemployment rate were 10 percent, you could attract all the candidates you wanted with a simple posting. There would be a sea of job seekers to pick from. But as long as the job market is competitive, you need to build relationships with passive candidates. That means every day. In reality, how difficult would it really be to pick up the phone and talk to one candidate per day? This doesn't mean doing an interview on every call. It only means making contact and engaging in a ten-minute conversation.

One of my coaching clients, Joe, runs a small but successful financial planning company. About a year ago, one of his employees, Peter, left for another position. Joe found out recently from Peter's parents that he was unhappy with his new job. I suggested that Joe pick up the telephone and contact Peter for a short conversation. Joe pushed back and said he was unwilling; it would seem like begging. I insisted that he just keep in contact. Peter always looked up to Joe as a mentor. All he would have to do is ask Peter how things were going and mention, if appropriate, that he heard Peter wasn't happy where he was. Then just let Peter talk. In reality, that's all you really have to do: just keep in contact with passive job seekers and maintain a relationship. Start the conversation, ask how things are going, and just listen.

Magic happens when you listen. Decades ago, I bought a new handheld Pilot Pen. This was the precursor of handheld CRM databases. It was an early database record keeper about the size of a cell phone. I painstakingly keyed in nearly five hundred names and contact information. I wanted to have them readily available without opening my computer. Weeks went by before I finally decided to try this new gadget out. During a two-hour layover in Minneapolis, I put 25 cents in a pay phone (which shows you how long ago this was). I dialed the first Minnesota telephone number I could find.

It was a past client I had not talked to in two years. I simply started a conversation to let my client know I was stuck at the airport and wanted to catch up. He immediately offered to take me out to dinner. When I told him I didn't have that much time, we got back to business. He just spoke to the president of his company a few weeks ago and learned they were having a leaders' conference in six months. He was in charge of picking speakers and asked if I was available on that date. He didn't ask about speaking fees, topics, or even airfare costs. He just booked me on the spot. I'm a big believer in relationships and an even bigger proponent of making them consistent. If you could build stronger relationships with clients or customers, you would generate more business. If you could build stronger and more consistent relationships with passive candidates, you would never again struggle to find good people.

Passive candidates should always be your focus. These folks are not motivated to change jobs but are certainly interested in talking. Passive candidates need to be recruited, because they won't usually respond to normal job postings. Life is good enough right now, but not what they want in the long term. They are always interested in "great."

RECRUITING PASSIVE CANDIDATES WITH NOMINATORS

The best way to recruit is to use *nominators*, or center of influence contacts. These are people whose evaluation skills you trust. They also conduct interviews and may be willing to share contact information for those they interviewed but didn't hire.

My definition of a great recruiter is someone who has the ability to use a headhunting firm but never has to. Headhunters may be great at the executive C-suite jobs, but are a waste of money at the administrative levels. You will spend between $3,000 and $10,000 for the headhunter, but you still have to interview candidates and make hiring decisions, whether you use a firm or do it yourself. All these firms are doing is tracking down candidates for you to interview. You now have the skills to recruit effectively, without paying all that money.

The other downside of using a recruiting firm is their guarantee. Most of them will guarantee a new hire for only six months to one year. If your new hire leaves just after one year, you are out a lot of money. I mentioned earlier that I was told by a candidate that she made an agreement with the recruiter to stay one year, no matter how much she hated the job. She left after one year and a day.

An effective way of finding passive candidates is developing a network of nominators. These are contacts who can introduce you to great people. Most managers will interview a few candidates before making a decision. Often managers throw a coin in the air in the selection process. They are just guessing. Some candidates are so good that the employer doesn't know whom to pick. This is where you come in. Your job is to keep in contact with these nominators. The purpose of nominators is only to introduce you to potential candidates. Even if you have an acquaintance relationship, the minimum interval to talk to nominators should be every three months.

Nominators can be colleagues in nearby branches, friends who might be managers in other companies, small business owners, professionals like CPAs and attorneys, as well as HR managers for large companies. All of these professionals can be recruiting sources for your next hire. The added benefit is that you will also develop more business contacts and possibly make more sales. People tend to buy from people they trust. Those they trust the most are usually the ones they contact most frequently. There is no downside to these calls. Even if the nominator doesn't know anybody, you have jogged their memory. The worst that could happen is a more solid relationship that may bear fruit in the future.

Another reason to keep and nurture a nominator network is to mine their contacts. Even though they don't have a job opening, they may have met someone who could be good in the future.

As you meet friends and contacts throughout the week, let them know about your job openings. If you don't have a ready opportunity, let them know about the kind of people you are always interested in.

One key point in talking to nominators is not to ask if they know anybody who needs a job. First, they won't know. Secondly, if you ask if they know somebody, they will immediately access their memories of the past week. If they can't remember somebody who asked for a job in the last seven days, they will again have amnesia.

The real trick here is to ask whom they know who would be good at the job. Whom do they know with the skills and personality to be successful? It's critical to mention that you are not looking for someone who needs a job. That's always what the nominator will mistakenly hear. Emphasize that you are looking for somebody who could be good at the job even though they may be currently employed. If you can make that plain, it will change everything.

The nominator strategy is taken from the referral lead generation approach in sales. Most salespeople fail in getting referrals because they ask whom the client knows they should be talking to. Often, they say, "Whom do you know who could use my services?" What they should ask instead is, "Whom do you know who could benefit from my services?" The second sentence makes all the difference. You always want the listener to be thinking, is there anybody who could benefit from working with you? This is the same mindset you want the nominator to have. Anybody with the skills and communication ability that you require could benefit by working with you.

A CONVERSATION WITH NOMINATORS

MANAGER: I have a job opening for a stable, organized, articulate administrative assistant. As you know, our

benefits are first-rate. Our pay is competitive. Who do you
know who could be effective at this job?

NOMINATOR: I don't know anybody who is looking for a job
as an administrative assistant. But if I do, I will keep you
in mind.

MANAGER: I'm not really looking for somebody who needs
a job. The unemployment rate right now is super low. Yet
83 percent of the people with jobs don't like what they're
doing. In fact, they even may be passively looking for
a new opportunity. I'm looking for somebody who you
think might be effective at this job. Who do you know
who could be good?

Did you notice that the manager didn't let the nominator become distracted? The manager didn't ask who needed a
job; instead, he asked who could be good, whether they were
employed or not. This is a trait of a great recruiter. They are
always asking who could be good instead of who is available.
They are always looking. They are always interested in meeting
great people.

Here we are looking for a nominator's database. Whom do
they know who might be good? Who has impressed them in recent
memory? You might even get lucky when the nominator gives you
a name of someone they interviewed but, for whatever reason,
didn't hire. Whenever I hire a new person in my company, there
are always two or three candidates who could have been good. I
simply chose the person I thought was best.

Mistakes Recruiters Make

Another mistake working with nominators is failing to get a name. Often the nominator will say, *"One person comes to mind. I'll give them a call and ask if they want to talk to you."*

Don't let them make the call. It will always be, *"I know someone who is looking to hire someone. Shall I give them your name? Do you need a job?"*

If this was an active job seeker, the answer would be yes. But that could be a needle in a haystack. Great recruiters will always get the name of the candidate first. If the nominator wants to make an introductory phone call, so much the better. But you should never let a nominator sell the opportunity. That's your job.

This is the same strategy with referrals. Your client has a name of somebody you could help. They call the referred lead and ask their friend if they want to sell their house and talk to a realtor. They may not be ready and say no. Your referral source calls you back and says they are not ready to sell but will let you know. On the other hand, if you made the call and introduced yourself, you could find out more about their plans to move and when to call back. You could keep the new referred lead in your database and call every three months to catch up. When they were ready to sell, your frequent phone calls would end up being right time, right place. You would get their business. Never, ever depend on the nominator to sell the candidate for you. Your job is to always get a name and initiate contact yourself.

Great recruiters are great salespeople. They always keep passive candidates in the pipeline.

Great recruiters are not satisfied with only contacting active job seekers who have quit or about to be fired. They are looking for passive job seekers who would leave for a better opportunity. These are the folks who are good at what they do, but possibly dissatisfied where they're at. These candidates are fair game.

Some of your nominators may even be working for you. Many companies will post job openings and first offer interviews to existing employees. Some of them may wish to move up in the organization, while others may know friends and family who may want a better opportunity. Either way, you're getting solid recommendations from people you know. You are actually taking advantage of their existing network without having to source outside job boards, headhunting firms, or advertisements.

STAFF REFERRALS

During a recent speech to an electronics firm, I sat down at a table of HR directors and asked how they recruit. My speech was on advanced interview and communication techniques. I presented ways to spot lies and misdirection as well as insights into how to improve their emotional intelligence.

One HR manager offered $2,000 to any employee who recommended a new hire. While this may seem extravagant to you, the distribution of the money was innovative; $500 was paid on the hire; another $500 was paid if the candidate lasted six months. The balance of $1,000 was paid if the candidate could pass the one-year mark. The incentive could be gamed if the employee and the candidate collaborated. But that was worth the risk. This firm hired frequently and didn't have time to source candidates through job boards or the media. It was a wonderful system, which motivated employees to come up with candidates.

I spoke to the Utah Trucking Association recently. One owner said he gives his employees $500 for any qualified candidate who joins the firm. He started with $100, then went to $250, but got very few results. The magic number to motivate staff seems to be $500. I'm sure that $1,000 would also work, but would probably be unnecessary.

The Halo Effect

In my company, we hire infrequently. The last two staff members I employed came from recommendations from current employees. There is a little bit of a halo effect when a referral comes from someone you trust. The halo effect also occurs with very attractive candidates. Because of their appearance and conduct, we tend to believe they have a better work ethic and more intelligence and motivation than the less attractive.

Internal employees are not the only way to source candidates. I'm a former member of Palisades Tennis Club in Newport Beach, California. Years ago the owner, Ken Stuart, came up with an idea to compensate members for introducing new prospects to the club. He offered $200 for each member who recommended someone who joined. At the time, I was playing with a Thursday night group of eight guys who were not members. We would go out to eat after the evening tennis and I would chat up a couple of the players. I joked with each of my friends that I would make $200 off them. I also offered to share the referral fee by buying them beer. Two of them wound up joining the club.

The point is that your customers may be a wonderful source of new candidates. You could offer top-tier customers money, discounts, or even token rewards like a dinner for two at a fancy restaurant. Since they know your business so well, customers and clients are great sources of referrals. While I have never seen major companies like American Airlines, IBM, Oracle, or Facebook advertise job openings to customers, I have seen many smaller companies ask customers or clients whom they would recommend.

Three Steps in Gaining Nominator Referrals

Here's a three-step process in working with nominators to source great candidates.

1. CALL THE NOMINATOR ON A FREQUENT BASIS.

Let them know the type of person you are looking for. Describe the job and the traits. Ask the nominator if they have interviewed anybody like that or know anyone who could be good. Don't depend on the nominator to contact the candidate for you. The nominator will only ask the candidate if they are looking for a job.

The best candidates are probably already working. Most of us are in jobs we don't like. You will be surprised how many are willing to interview for a better opportunity. It's really important to avoid letting the nominator call for you. What they will probably say is, "I know somebody who has a job opening. Shall I have them call you?" The response will always be, "I already have a job." The nominator will then say the candidate isn't interested. Nominators will be the worst salespeople. If they want to send an introductory e-mail to the candidate, encourage them. But don't let them sell for you.

2. FIND OUT SOMETHING PERSONAL ABOUT THE CANDIDATE.

Do they play golf or tennis? How many kids do they have? How did they meet their spouse? These personal details will streamline your phone calls. A mortgage broker called me twelve years ago. He had been referred by my lawyer. He said "I heard you were a professional tennis player in the 1970s. Did you play Jimmy Connors?" He and I talked for about twenty minutes about tennis and what life was like on the tour. He bought time on the phone and booked an appointment.

3. LISTEN FOR CANDIDATES.

Nominators always talk about their friends and contacts. All you have to do is listen for names and ask questions. If you get good at listening, you will never have to ask for candidates' names again.

You may be asking, "Once I get the name of a candidate, what am I supposed to say?" Here's another process you can use in that conversation.

The Five-Step Referred Candidate Script

1. INTRODUCE YOURSELF AND GIVE THE NAME OF YOUR COMPANY AND REFERRAL SOURCE.

Hi, my name is Kerry Johnson with IPS. We have a mutual friend, John Thompson. You know John, don't you?

It's important to engage with the candidate in the first seven seconds. Get them to respond. But never pitch. Don't sell the job. Listen them into the job.

2. USE THE PERSONAL TOUCH.

John tells me that you are a scratch golfer. Congratulations! How long have you been playing golf?

This simple reference to their personal life will gain you ten more minutes on the phone. Now you have become a friend of a friend.

3. ESTABLISH YOUR BRAND: GIVE THE ELEVATOR SPEECH.

The next step is using an elevator speech. This is a sixty-second introduction to who you are and what you do. It's especially useful with referrals and recruiting. The elevator speech is critical in framing the conversation. The candidate has been introduced and knows your name. They have also noticed that you've paid enough attention to know something special about them. But they are still curious about who you are and what you do. This is where the elevator speech comes in.

Here are three ways to create a killer elevator speech.

1. Label yourself in one sentence or less. You can use the elevator speech any time, in any situation. You can use it at a party, a networking meeting, a bar or even a church. A great entrée to do an elevator speech is when somebody says, what do you do? Tell the listener your name and your position in the company.

When you are in a referred lead conversation, the most elegant way to begin an elevator speech is, "Did Don say anything about me? Can I give you a quick elevator speech?" Since nearly everyone in business knows what this is (although few know how to do it), they would love to hear yours.

2. Tell the listeners three things that you do better than anybody on earth. These benefits need to be short, succinct, and impressive. They can be benefits you provide or your company can give. Instead of saying, "We are a real estate company that helps home-buyers and sellers," you might instead say, "We are a real estate company that does three things:

- "We help sellers get the highest price possible on their property.
- "We help our sellers move within ninety days.
- "Because of our superior negotiating skills, our buyers usually end up paying 10 percent below comparable properties."

One of my financial planning coaching clients says he does three things:

- Helps clients get above market performance with below market risk.

- Helps clients make sure their retirement funds never run out before they do.
- Makes sure his clients sleep at night by decreasing investment volatility.

3. Tell a story illustrating the three things you do. Using a story to illustrate benefits during the elevator speech is crucial. Most people will quickly forget what you do. But they will all remember a story.

Let's take a real estate elevator speech as an example. One of my coaching clients says that he can sell a property in ninety days and get top dollar. He can also help his buyers negotiate a much better deal on their dream house than anybody else because of his negotiating skills.

Here's a story of how he illustrates each of these three benefits with a story.

A seller called me recently to list his house. He had a time crunch, since his new job started in a different state in forty-five days. He also only had about $50,000 equity in the house. We listed the property at a fair price based on the comps. But to ensure a fast sale, we rented furniture to really dress the house up. With new paint inside and out, we also fixed cracks in the brick and walkways. This only took a few days but made the house look even better than all the other homes for sale. A qualified prospect came by three weeks after the listing and fell in love with the property. Although it took us three days to negotiate the price, we were also able to work with the mortgage company on the buyer side to allow a thirty-day move-in. The seller had a two-week buffer before they had to move to start a new job. This is exactly what I try to do with every buyer and seller I work with.

Let's apply the elevator speech concept to recruiting, using the same real estate example.

As you know, my name is Don Smith, and I own Smith Real Estate. We do three things for our clients. First, we help our sellers get top dollar and move within ninety days. Second, we help our buyers get a better deal because of our ability to negotiate. But most importantly, we do constant skill training and pay a competitive salary. In fact, we produce more than nearly all our competitors. And we always help our staff work towards their long-term career goals.

One of our administrative folks decided they wanted to become a sales producer. We paid for the licensing and training. Because of our experience, we helped her make $150,000 within eighteen months. We did this because of extensive training, our great lead origination, and competitive technology. We try to help everyone hit their career goals. This is why our staff retention is so good. We never lose people to the competition.

I encourage you to create your own elevator speech immediately. Do one for recruiting and a personal one for describing yourself. For example, I have an elevator speech for the speaking part of my business as well as one for my coaching activity.

Here's my speaking elevator speech:

I'm a best-selling author and an MBA, PhD-level business psychologist. I speak around the world on topics like how to read your client's mind, how to increase your business by 80 percent within eight weeks, and how to hire recruit and retain great people.

About five years ago I spoke at the Million Dollar Round Table in Vancouver, British Columbia on how to read your client's mind. The day after my speech, one attendee walked up and said, "That touching below the elbow thing really works." I said, "How do you know?" He went to Cardrina's restaurant the night after my presentation. A server was aimlessly walking around with a tray of tequila shooters. The guy walked up and said, "Are you having some problems tonight?" She said, "Nobody wants tequila." He said, "I just heard a speaker today talk about touching people on the arm. Why don't you walk over to that guy at the second table, touch him on the arm, and ask if he wants to buy a glass of tequila?" She said, "I'm not going to touch anybody." My attendee said, "Nothing else is working; why don't you give it a try?"

She walked over, touched the customer below the elbow, and asked whether he wanted to buy a tequila for himself or a round for the whole table. She had the whole tray sold in ten minutes. She walked over to a beautiful bay front window and put the tray down. The attendee who heard me speak said, "Did it work?" She said, "Really well." He said, "Why don't you get another tray?" She said, "I don't want to do it anymore. It worked too well. I think it's unethical!"

My elevator speech is so effective because I illustrate the "touching below the elbow" segment of the "How to read your client's mind" speech with a story. It's really easy to forget my bullet points but very difficult to forget the story. It's important to use a story during all of your elevator speeches. Make sure that stories illustrate what you do or what your company does. You will not only get attention but will also gain engagement with the job candidate you are trying to attract.

Here's another example of my coaching elevator speech. It's different from what I use when selling speeches.

I am a best-selling author and an MBA, PhD-level business psychologist. I do three things in my coaching practice. First, I help clients create a business plan that nearly always increases production by 80 percent within just a few months. Second, we rebuild basic skills so my clients can work fewer hours. Third, we help them build advanced skills so they can hit their long-term goals much more quickly than they could on their own.

One of my clients, Matt, runs a successful mortgage company. He has ten employees, and he desperately needed management training as well as increased sales performance. First, we identified the sales goals he needed to achieve his personal income goals. Second, we put together a systematic sales process to close more deals. Third, we implemented management systems to improve his whole team's performance. After three months, his sales increased by 80 percent. After one year, his management skills, including communication with his team, improved performance by 35 percent. Matt is not unique. He only wanted to improve his business and his skills more quickly than he could on his own.

4. USE BENEFITS AND TAKEAWAYS.

Again, we never want to pitch the job opportunity. We always want to "listen" people into an opportunity. But it's important to start with a benefit and provide a takeaway. For example, "I run a successful consulting company. I'm looking for someone to book me as a speaker. It requires great sales skills. The pay is competitive, and you would be working in a business-to-business environment."

Here comes the takeaway. "I'm not sure if this is the right opportunity for you, but I would love to ask a few questions to find out more. Is there a chance we can talk?" Sometimes candidates will say they already have a job. Your response needs to be, "If you did not have a job, we probably wouldn't be talking," but add, "I'd like to find out more about you to see if this can be an opportunity." Very few will blow you off the telephone.

5. QUALIFY THE CANDIDATE.

At this point, you need to do a short interview asking about their skills and experience. Try to find out within ten minutes what they do. You are listening for energy and past successful performance. You can always train for skills. If you like what you hear, schedule a face-to-face meeting. At that meeting, you can apply your interview skills.

The Wedge:
How to Motivate Candidates to Say Yes

I am often asked what to say to a candidate who is happy with their current employer. This is probably a reflex response, which suggests you've pitched the job opportunity too fast. Reflex responses occur often in retail. Let's say you walk into a clothing store to buy a long-sleeved button-down shirt. The salesperson asks, "Can I help you?" Your unconscious reflex response is, "No, I'm just looking." You may even wonder why you said that, since you actually needed some help.

Your candidates will behave the same way. You might tell them about the job opportunity too quickly, to which you will get the response that they are happy where they are working. Most recruiters would end the conversation immediately, thinking the referral is actually not a qualified candidate. But you know from reading this book that prescription without diagnosis is malpractice. It's critical to get to know the person before you pitch anything.

If you use the prescribed referred lead approach of introducing yourself, three things you and your company do, the takeaway, and the five-step bridge (a technique similar to what I have described as the five-step referred candidate script), you'll never make the mistake of pitching too quickly and getting a reflex response.

A much better technique is to use the *wedge*. This is an elegant way of finding out why someone joined a company and what would it take to make their job and career path better. You are driving a wedge between them and their employer, trying to find out what it would take to make a change to your company.

The Wedge: Three Steps
1. INSTANT REPLAY.

Ask why the person joined their employer. (We will dig deeper into this question during the interview stage of the selection process later in this book.) An especially valuable question is to ask how someone decided to join a company.

In seminars I hammer the point that except for the grace of God, who can change anybody's heart, people don't change. We are the same today as ten years ago, except for a new car, new hairstyle, and possibly a new house.

The recidivism rate—that is, the percentage of felons who commit the same crime again—is 83 percent within three years of release. The divorce rate in America is nearly 62 percent within ten years. Guess what the second-marriage divorce rate is? Higher or lower? The second-marriage divorce rate is 78 percent within ten years. I jokingly say that second-marriage divorce rates are so high because you took yourself with you into the second marriage.

Curiously, third-marriage divorce rates are at about 36 percent. These folks tend to be in their fifties and sixties. They also realize that they made serious mistakes in the past and won't do the same in the future.

I believe that major events like religious conversion, war, and sometimes loss of valuable relationships can effect change. But generally, most people don't change. If you grant that, you must also grant that how people made decisions in the past is likely to be the way they make future ones. If you can find out how a candidate picked their last job, you will probably understand the mental strategy they will use in the future.

Simply ask, "How did you decide to pick your current job?"

You might have to dig a little deeper into the response. They may tell you about the relationship with the owner or a friend in the company. They will likely tell you about how they learned about the job opening. None of that is useful to a recruiter. You simply want to learn how they made the decision. You will probably hear reasons like:

- The health benefits were really impressive.
- The training program and the college reimbursement were the reason.
- They promised advancement in the company within one year.

These are the reasons people often select jobs. If your candidate selected their current position based on these reasons (or others), they will likely decide to join your company based on the same ones.

2. LISTEN FOR FRICTION POINTS.

It is really important to get people to talk. You want to hear what they like about their current job as well as what they don't. You want to hear about frustrations, unfulfilled promises, and dreams they still aspire to. But more importantly, which of these would they like to change and improve? There are few candidates who would not like to find something to improve. It could be hours, pay, benefits, training, or advancement. There are very few people who are satisfied and comfortable. There are also few who have no desire to improve anything.

3. ASK THE "LET'S ASSUME" QUESTION.

This is probably the most powerful recruiting technique you will ever learn. Most recruiters will pitch their job and see if there's any interest. The more elegant recruiters will listen to what a candidate wants in the long term. But very few recruiters know what to ask. Now you do.

This question is designed to tell you three things the candidate wants most in moving to a new position. This perfect question is, "Let's assume it's ten years in the future. What happened that let you know it was the perfect job and you had a great boss?"

The magic comes in how you ask the question. Since most candidates probably have never been asked this, they may at first seem confused. Just restate the question. "Let's assume it's ten years in the future. Looking backwards to today, what did you experience that let you know the position was perfect for you and you had a great relationship with your manager?"

I am excited about this question because of its elegance. It helps the candidate become more conversational and tell you exactly what they want. All you have to do then is present the position according to what the candidate is looking for. Obviously, if what they have is better than what you are offering, you need to be more competitive.

Obviously, you would only pose this question to someone who is qualified. But with a low unemployment rate, it's not only important to source qualified candidates but also to attract them to the next step in the interview process if you think they are good. This question does it.

There are three parts to the "let's assume" technique:

1. Listen for three needs. It will be very tempting for you to listen for one need and then talk about how your company will be the solution. Resist this temptation to talk. One professional recruiter told me the story of a candidate he sent to a company. The president asked the candidate what he looked forward to. The candidate only got one sentence out when the president interrupted. He spoke about how long the company had been in business, their vision over the next couple years, how wonderful their employees are, and how great their compensation plan is. After the one-hour meeting, the candidate left. The president told the recruiter how impressed he was by the candidate. As you would suspect, the candidate took another job. The president was trying to sell the candidate instead of trying to find out if the candidate was the right person. Always listen. You need to find out their needs.

2. Quantify their emotions. Most of the time candidates will talk about their desire for opportunities. They will talk about goals and where they want to be in the next few years. They may even be philosophical and talk about a job that inspires, motivates, and is significant. The problem is apples and oranges. Their definition of inspiration may be different than what the job provides. You need to drill the answers down.

RECRUITER: What does *inspire* mean to you?

CANDIDATE: It means looking forward to going to work in the morning.

RECRUITER: In the past, what has made you look forward to going to work in the morning?

CANDIDATE: A project that I know will make money for the company and me and that we can successfully complete.

RECRUITER: How much money?

CANDIDATE: My last project earned a $5,000 bonus. That was pretty motivating.

RECRUITER: So, if I heard you correctly, you said inspiration means a project that will make you and the company money, but also generate a $5,000 bonus for you? Did I get that right?

You can see from this dialogue that it's not enough to ask the question. You have to probe and have enough emotional intelligence to listen for meaning and intent. It's also critical to communicate in the same emotional language. As you can see, the word *inspire* may mean something totally different to the candidate than to you. Defining the meaning of what they say and quantifying it, if possible, will help you do a much better job in getting the right candidate to join your company.

Most poor hires are due to miscommunication during the interview. What you expect is not what the candidate can deliver. Because of this "apples and oranges" conversation, whom you thought you hired is not whom you got. It's the same for the candidate. It's critical to find out the meaning and intent of what they said, instead of just listening to their words.

3. Recap and trial-close. Once you hear needs and quantify emotions, it's important to recap and then trial-close.

In the above example, you heard the candidate describe inspiration as working on a project that makes money for the company and the candidate. The candidate went on to say that inspiration meant a $5,000 bonus. The way you would recap all of that would be by saying:

"If I heard you correctly, you said you want to be inspired, meaning that you want to work on projects that make money for the company and you. *Inspiring* means that you would make a bonus of $5,000. Did I get that right?"

A trial close is just getting the candidate to commit to the solution: "So if we could talk about projects that make money for the company and earn you $5,000, would that be helpful?" Or you could say, "If we could explore ways of helping you do inspiring projects that make money for you and the company and also pay you a $5,000 bonus, would that be a worthwhile conversation?"

If they say yes to the trial close, you have somebody interested in exploring an opportunity. But even hearing a no is not that bad. If they say no, it only means you didn't listen very well. Just ask what you missed and do the "let's assume" question again.

Sometimes, you will hear people who only want to talk. They want to vent. They don't want to reach solutions. I was at my tennis club recently sharing a pitcher of beer with my doubles partner. He said, "You're a sort of a business psychologist, right?"

I said, "Yeah. Why?"

He said, "I have a salesperson who comes in late, leaves early, annoys the staff, and isn't hitting his goals."

I said, "Let me get this straight. Your sales guy comes in late, leaves early, annoys your staff, and is still not hitting his performance goals. Did I get that right?"

My partner said, "Absolutely, and it ticks me off."

But then I did a trial close to see if he was interested in the solution. I said, "So if we could take a look at what to do with this guy, would that be helpful?"

My partner looked at his beer for a long time, and then back to me saying, "Nope. I got it. Pass the pitcher!"

This is a good example of listening to someone who wants to vent their emotions but does not want a solution. When you listen for three needs using the "let's assume" technique, make sure you always recap what they said. But most importantly, trial-close to make sure they're committed to working on a solution.

Here's a sample dialogue of how you can use the wedge technique effectively.

CANDIDATE: I knew one of the company's salespeople from college.

RECRUITER: I'm really glad to hear that you knew people within the organization. But why that company? Why not somebody else? What did they offer that really attracted you?

CANDIDATE: It was the MBA training reimbursement that really got me. They offered to reimburse me for any tuition costs within thirty days of completing each class.

I already have student debt and can't afford anymore. This was a big benefit for me.

RECRUITER: I heard you say the word *was*. Did you complete your MBA?

CANDIDATE: No. I haven't had time. I've been working eighteen-hour days, with barely enough time to sleep.

RECRUITER: Wow! It sounds like you're working very hard. What frustrates you the most in your current job? What would you like to see changed?

CANDIDATE: We are really understaffed. I was promised that these eighteen-hour days would only be a few months. But it is now going on nearly a year. I was promised an MBA reimbursement, but don't even have the time to take advantage of it.

RECRUITER: I'm hearing a lot of frustrations. But here's a very tough question: let's assume it's ten years in the future. What happened during those ten years to let you know you have the perfect job and a great relationship with your coworkers and managers?

CANDIDATE: I don't understand the question. It hasn't been ten years yet.

RECRUITER: I understand. But put yourself in the future ten years from now. Looking backwards to today, what did you get that let you know the job was a great place to work and your manager was excellent?

CANDIDATE: I guess there was some career advancement and a chance to increase my income, and my manager encouraged and coached me instead of just telling me what I did wrong.

RECRUITER: What does *career advancement* mean?

CANDIDATE: It means the MBA reimbursement benefit that I was offered but never got a chance to use.

RECRUITER: You said increase your income. How much?

CANDIDATE: If I could get a 10 percent increase in my income per year depending on job performance, that would be great.

RECRUITER: You mentioned that your manager was encouraging and coached you. What does that mean?

CANDIDATE: My current manager usually tells me what I messed up on. I would rather hear what I'm doing well and suggestions on how to do things better. I usually end up feeling berated instead of encouraged.

RECRUITER: If I heard you correctly, you said a perfect job would involve career advancement. This means the same MBA reimbursement program you had with your previous job. You also said a chance to increase your income. Meaning that based on job performance, your income would increase by 10 percent per year. Lastly, your manager would be encouraging and coaching. This means helping you get things done better instead of just berating you. Did I get all that right?

CANDIDATE: Absolutely. That sounds exactly right.

RECRUITER: If we could talk about hitting these goals, would that be beneficial?

CANDIDATE: Yes. I can't wait to talk about it.

The wedge technique not only helps you find out why someone picked a previous job and what they would like to improve in their current job, but also what they would like to see in a perfect job. When you can find these three pieces of information, you can then match your job presentation to the person you're talking to. It's not enough to find someone who is qualified. You also have to find a great candidate who will tell you what it will take for them to join your company.

Why Now Is Such a Good Time to Recruit!

We know that 83 percent of the population don't like what they do and are actively looking for another opportunity, and 69 percent would consider leaving if they found something better. Keeping a database of passive job seekers will keep your company staffed for years to come with the right people. But if you're not using these kinds of sourcing techniques, you will get shut down as soon as you hear, "I already have a job."

Fire Employees to Boost Your Business

You may be thinking that you have no openings in your company. Until you have a need, why spend time talking to candidates? You should always be recruiting. The truth is, you have employees that either don't want to be there or are doing less than their best. If they are not supporting your goals and vision, they are a drag to those aspirations. Don't employ people who are not trying their hardest.

I played professional tennis from 1976 until 1978. I jokingly say that I was ranked number 95 in the world until they fixed the ATP computer ranking system, whereby I slipped to 10,033. I was a better doubles player than singles. I also had better results in doubles, although I made less money. It's common to watch your partner hit a bad shot and say, "I guess it's three against one today." In fact your partner is always playing his best. But what if he isn't? What if he purposely hits balls into the net, misses shots wide, and double-faults? What if he is not trying to win? Would you keep playing with the same partner? Would you dump your doubles partner for a chance of winning in the future?

Your business team is like a tennis doubles team. If you can't win, why continue to play with the same partner? In my decades of speaking and coaching to companies around the world, I have rarely seen anyone fired at the perfect time. Generally, the companies I work with segment their teams in three areas:

1. **A third of your employees are superstars.** They are trying as hard as they can to be successful and support the team. They are also learning and developing skills to better perform the job.

2. **A third of your employees are just getting by.** They are doing what they have to do to survive. They won't do anything heroic or above and beyond. They aren't concerned about becoming more competitive or help the team. They are doing just enough to stay employed. They're not giving any manager reason to terminate them. They are getting the job done, but not much else.

3. **The last third should be terminated.** They don't respond to instruction. They make no effort to improve. They also may whine and complain about any new effort at development. They will put themselves first before the organization and cut corners when they can. They refuse to grow and will be a drag on your company and profits.

One of my clients has an assistant who should have been let go years ago. She is polite enough on the telephone. She is effective enough handling basic administrative duties. But she is not good enough in any one area to help my client get to the next level. My client takes administration work home at night. He calls clients to reschedule and follow up with his own paperwork—all things the assistant should do. My client rationalizes that she is probably overworked. At times, he admits she should be replaced with someone better. But he can't bring himself to do it. I even ask if he would feel better finding another job for her. Even that would not make him pull the trigger.

Another client runs a small company. She is always at the edge of making or losing money depending on the month. Her assistant displays the same behaviors. I worked with her on a one-on-one basis for about four coaching sessions. I even gave her a script on how her assistant should answer the telephone. I produced another script helping book telephone appointments. The assistant responded well for about one week and reverted to her old behavior. The problem is that she still works there.

One of my MBA graduate school leadership professors once said, "Don't keep people who won't share or work to achieve your vision." I certainly believe that but would also add, "We need to terminate people who can't or won't learn." If you have an employee who does a good job, you are lucky. Often as we move folks up to higher levels, they have to learn to be effective at the new position. The skill set and the attitude necessary for a more advanced position needs to be developed. There are two options you have for those who can't and often won't learn. Either move them to a different seat on the bus, as Jim Collins suggests, or terminate them and search for someone who can and will perform.

A good example is President Abraham Lincoln during the Civil War. He managed not only to win the war but also to keep a divided country together. One of his management secrets was hiring a cabinet of rivals. His secretary of state was William Seward. The secretary of the treasury was Salmon P. Chase. His secretary of war was Edwin Stanton, and the attorney general was James Speed. They were all rivals with differing opinions and viewpoints, but they were all required to support Lincoln's vision and mission. Lincoln's selection was based on their diverse opinions and viewpoints. But he retained them because of their support and effectiveness toward his policies, goals, and missions.

Ulysses S. Grant was perhaps Lincoln's greatest general. He tapped Grant in 1864, promoting him from major general to commander of the whole Union Army. He also picked William Tecumseh Sherman to serve under Grant. All shared Lincoln's vision to preserve the Union and eradicate slavery.

One general did not share Lincoln's vision. He wouldn't take direction from his superiors. That general was George McClellan, commander of the Army of the Potomac. Despite orders to march,

McClellan would often retreat when a clear victory was within reach. Lincoln appropriately fired him. McClellan ran against Lincoln during the presidential election of 1864, and Lincoln easily defeated him.

One of my clients has a salesperson, Don, who does the minimum. Don barely prospects for new business and earns only enough to retain medical benefits. My client is trying to grow but is unwilling to fire Don. He finally decided to marginalize Don instead of firing this bottom third-tier producer. It took a month for my client to muster the fortitude to even do that.

It's Harder to Fire than Hire

It is really difficult to terminate anyone. It is much easier to hire somebody than fire them. But if you want your business to get to the next level, you have to get rid of those holding you back. Your employees need to strive to become part of the solution. If they are constantly the problem, let them go.

Fifteen years ago, I employed an office manager who talked a big game. He was recommended by a nominator I trusted. Because of the stellar recommendation, I didn't call past employers and didn't interview using the skills we have discussed. I hired him without doing my due diligence. After three months, two members of my staff complained about his hours and his condescension toward them. He rarely came to the office when I wasn't in town. He even ordered my staff to do his personal errands. I reprimanded him but was shy about firing.

At a presentation in New Orleans, my books and handouts hadn't been delivered. It was a Saturday, but I called his home. His new wife answered and said he wouldn't talk to me on a weekend. I needed to call back on Monday during office hours. I asked if she knew who I was. She said yes. I then said, "Tell him if he doesn't come to the phone now, he doesn't need to come into work on Monday." He didn't, and I fired him. The lesson is, "Hire slow. Fire fast." Who is working for you right now who shouldn't be there? Who is holding you and your team back?

Take a few minutes now and list your staff on a sheet of paper. Put an A, B, or C next to their names, corresponding to the segmentation I suggested earlier. Your C staff should be terminated or moved to other positions where they can excel. Your B staff are a much tougher decision. You need to take a serious look at whether you can find better people, or at least develop them into A's. Don't let a laissez-faire management style cause you to do nothing. The C's and possibly even the B's are holding your business back.

3

How to Interview

Have you ever made a wrong hire? Have you selected someone based on a great interview only to discover your hire turned out to be a different person than the one you interviewed?

The Five Biggest Hiring Mistakes You Will Ever Make

Interviewing is a lot like dating. You are looking for someone special, so you tend to find it. Whether that person is actually special or not is irrelevant. You've been on many social dates where you knew in the first five minutes whether the person was a match. But you probably weren't so desperate on social dates that you accepted anyone. Hopefully while you were waiting for Mr. Right, you didn't settle for Mr. Right Now. So why do we in business become so desperate to find somebody that we compromise our standards? Why do we accept somebody just good enough instead taking enough time to find the right person? Why not Mr. Right Hire instead of Mr. Right Now?

Here are five mistakes that most recruiters make.

1. FAILING TO BELIEVE PEOPLE WHEN THEY SHOW YOU WHO THEY ARE

Interviewers often make the mistake of thinking that candidates can and will change. They did not perform in the last job, but that only means they didn't have the right opportunity. But with your company, they can and will be successful! Because you and your organization have the special sauce that will create success for anyone.

Because interviewers are so desperate to fill a position, they sometimes rationalize and gloss over obvious past problems. These could be personal conflicts with other employees, or even customers.

Solution: If you can't find a good person, hire the best one you can find. Accept the whole package with eyes wide open. If a candidate has past problems, they will replicate them in the future. Don't assume they can or will change. If you know someone has had conflicts with past supervisors, you could commit to managing the candidate on your own. If attendance has been a past issue, you could give the candidate flexible hours, holding them accountable for production, not time. If a recruit has had previous problems communicating, isolate them from other staff. There are many things you can do to mitigate the problems people have had in the past. If you can't get the whole package, make adjustments with the parts that are necessary. But don't think they will change. Hope is always eternal. There are exceptions. But don't bet your business on it.

One of my clients, Joe, had a sales colleague who irritated nearly everybody in the office: she wouldn't prospect enough, she failed to communicate adequately, and she said inappropriate things to both customers and clients. In the beginning, she turned out to be a hiring mistake, but she did some things well. Joe moved her to a new seat on the bus instead of terminating her. He found an administrative worker who thrived.

2. HIRING SKILLS BEFORE ATTITUDE

Skills and knowledge are worthless without the motivation to implement them. Experience is also minimized if it is not shared with others. The smaller your business, the more jack-of-all-trades expertise you probably have. Transferring your skills to other members of the team is challenging, but not impossible. Later in this book we will talk about how to train people effectively.

But you can't train enthusiasm. You can train interpersonal skills, but you can't train people to be personable. You can train people to listen, but you can't train them to be empathetic. You can train people to show up, but you can't train them to be motivated when they arrive.

Many years ago, I was coaching a sales team of twelve producers. Our process to make lasting changes was to present a concept, illustrate it, role-play it, and then role-play it again the next week. I can usually get people to learn a process. But it is often difficult for them to change their mindset and apply it during the actual sales process.

During one role-play, Peter was practicing a trial close with his colleague Jeff. Peter said, "If we could work on the solution, would that be a benefit?"

Jeff said in response, "I guess."

I asked Peter what he thought Jeff meant. He said Jeff agreed. I asked Jeff what he meant by saying, "I guess." Jeff said he heard Peter but didn't really want to work on finding a solution.

This is an example of training somebody what to say without having enough emotional intelligence to notice what was meant. Peter missed the inflection, pace, pitch, tone, and rhythm of the message. These interpersonal skills are difficult to teach. If you could select somebody with a good attitude, motivation, curiosity, enthusiasm, and ambition, you can teach the skills later.

3. SELLING THE JOB INSTEAD OF LISTENING TO THE CANDIDATE

While you need to inspire candidates, you shouldn't sell them. It used to be said that great producers can sell ice cubes to Eskimos. This idea is very glib. Today, glib isn't enough. Sales resistance is so intense that even engaged candidates will feel manipulated.

A much better way to motivate a candidate is to present a one-minute elevator speech and just listen. You can talk about the opportunities the company has to match the candidate's goals. But the candidate should talk at a minimum three times as much as you. Good candidates have already done their homework. They looked at your website and LinkedIn presence and have possibly even chatted with current employees. Don't make your candidate feel they are doing you a favor by working for you. They will never perform at their best.

I live part-time in the small coastal town of Carvoeiro, in southern Portugal. I am there usually a month every quarter. It's a little village of 3,000 people at the very bottom of the Iberian Peninsula. We live in a two-bedroom cottage with a breathtaking view of the Atlantic. It's only a forty-five-minute hydrofoil ride from Morocco.

Down two flights of stairs from my house is the Atlantic View, a bar I can see from the roof of my terrace. The ownership changed hands a year ago along with new employees. I've gotten to know the employees fairly well. Nearly everyone who works there says they are trying to help the owner. Nearly every employee who says that seems to only go through the motions. There is no real effort to build the business.

During one night in June every year, our little town swells to 50,000. The event is called the Black-and-White Night, when the whole town dresses up in their favorite black-and-white outfits. One of the "I'm helping the owner out" employees was given a sign and asked to direct the passers-by up to the bar. He held the sign while texting. He was totally oblivious to the amount of business his "buy one get one free" advertisement offered.

These employees are hiring mistakes. The owner recruited them because she needed somebody and explained how to do the job. It was obvious they were not terribly interested in the opportunity. Their job was to collect a paycheck. Listening to the candidate's goals, aspirations, likes, and dislikes is critical in selecting the right person.

It's OK to hire a temp to fill in, but you must supervise them more than someone who cares. If all they are doing is showing up, make sure they are well led as they do it. Treat them as you would your own child, who said they would help you out.

Solution: Describe the business, position, and opportunity. Be factual, but don't embellish. If you do make a statement about the great opportunity available, use a takeaway phrase at the end, for example, "I'm not sure this is right for you, but I would like to hear more about your goals and needs first." Another example is, "We have leads that are so qualified that you may not have to prospect on your own ever again. In fact, most of our producers have doubled their income from the previous jobs. I'm not sure this kind of opportunity is right for you, but I would like to hear more about you and your goals first."

4. HIRING FRIENDS AND FAMILY

While they're the easiest to recruit, these types of employees are the toughest to fire. You may find a recommendation from a nominator about a friend who would be good for your position. Be careful about nominators who inflate the candidate's qualities.

It's even worse when you hire a relative, or if you hire a relative of an existing employee. If you really want to know what pushback means, hire a family member. They will rarely work as hard as nonfamily staff.

I made this mistake three times in my forty-plus-years career. I once hired a sister-in-law who argued with me so intensely that I eventually gave up trying to coach her. I asked my wife to be in the room when I fired her.

In the late 1980s, I hired a marketer named Joy, who brought in two of her best friends to work at my company. When Joy and I discussed her low sales production, she quit. Both of her friends also quit in sympathy. I lost my whole staff because their friendship was deeper than their commitment to me or the job. When my brother and I had a partnership that went south, we didn't talk for two years. My oldest daughter, Stacey, brought us back together. We are best friends now, but the argument against nepotism is pretty solid.

Solution: Don't hire family members. Hire employee acquaintances but not close friends. If you do hire family members, make sure they don't work together. If you hire one of your kids, tell them ahead of time how they could get terminated. Let them know that your expectations of them are the same as any other employee. I personally like managers who tell candidates how they can get fired. It's sort of like a prenuptial agreement without the house. Actually, you can talk about how they can get fired by talking about someone else who got fired. What did they do? What did it take to disappoint you?

5. NOT GOING ENOUGH WITH YOUR GUT

Often when we are desperate to fill a vacancy, we ignore intuition. We ignore the red flags raised during interviews. We rationalize poor performance with the hope of a better opportunity. Always consider your gut impressions as equally as you do salient qualities.

Some managers will take candidates on a tour through the operation. One of my clients told me a story recently how he will test a candidate. He will chat with an employee during a tour of the facilities, purposely ignoring the candidate's responses. If the candidate seems impatient or irritated by the interruption, that's a red flag.

Another manager will take a candidate to lunch. He will evaluate how the recruit talks to the servers as a way to see if there any other inconsistencies in his behavioral evaluation. One of my clients will play golf with candidates. He doesn't really care if the recruit has a low handicap. My client is trying to see if they will cheat. The manager is also trying to see if the candidate displays a temper and how quickly he can recover from a bad shot.

The comedian Bill Murray is featured adding up his golf shots in a TV commercial. "Let me see. The drive off the tee is one. Two in the trees. One out to the fairway. Two to the green. Three putts. Let me add that up. Make that a five." Probably not a good hire for an accounting job.

While these situations were all manufactured, it is better to find red flags during the courtship than after the wedding.

Solution: If in doubt, cross them out. If you see red flags in the beginning, they will only get worse in the end. If you doubt in any way a candidate's ability or their motivation to perform well, they will rarely surprise you after they are hired.

I have three daughters. All are attractive and smart. But the one piece of advice they never seem to get is what I call the "behavior magnification" principle. This means that anything you see that is slightly irritating in the beginning of a relationship will become intolerable later. The slightly endearing behavior of your boyfriend who brags about himself or the girlfriend who preens frequently becomes unbearable in time.

Most divorces are not due to spousal abuse, infidelity, or alcoholism. The biggest reason for marital breakups is irreconcilable differences. What you thought you were getting in the beginning is not what you ended up with. But the reality is that the person you courted didn't really change all that much. You just chose not to recognize bad behaviors in the beginning. You rationalized and romanticized poor behavior during the courtship "interview" process.

Interviewing Techniques That Will Help Pick the Right Person

How much does the interview impact your chances of hiring the right person? Seventy percent? Eighty percent? How about 2 percent?

According to a study done at the University of Michigan, your interview skills add only about a 2 percent greater chance of selecting great people than no interview at all. One of the reasons for the minimal result is that you tend to be attracted to people who are like you—even though the job would not be suited for you, or them.

For example, let's assume you have a job opening for an administrative assistant. This entails bookkeeping, light accounting, and a very organized mind. Yet you interview someone who is enthusiastic, engaging, and cares little about detail. Just like you—you become instantly attracted to this candidate, yet you are shocked when they don't work out. It is supremely difficult to make good hiring decisions based on the skill set required for the position. It is much better to let somebody else do the interviewing who has an affinity for the skills required, then talk to the person they recommend. That way, all you are really trying to do is assess their emotional intelligence and whether you can get along with them.

Candidates Have More Experience Interviewing than You

Candidates have interviewed more often than you. They are likely to say what you want to hear, not what you need to know in making informed hiring decisions. The candidate may interview twenty companies before they find a good fit. Each employer asks the same questions. The candidate knows exactly what is coming and is prepared for the answers you want to hear. Even if you recruit someone who's happily employed, your company is not the only one they have spoken to. On average, candidates will interview five or six possible employers.

This is especially difficult if your staff does the initial interviews. You may only interview once or twice every few years, while the candidate may have interviewed ten times that many. They have much more experience.

Many years ago, I was in the midst of hiring a new salesperson. I told my weekly Bible study group about the interview later that day. One of my friends at the study told me to ask a candidate, if they were a car, what model would they be? I thought that was a great question and later that day asked it.

The candidate said, "I bet you want me to say Porsche, because that would mean I was fast and flashy. If I said Volkswagen, that would mean I am sturdy and dependable. Which car should I be?" I realized right there this guy had much more experience interviewing than me. All the questions I could think of he had already been asked and had the answers for.

Another reason the interview doesn't help much is that 73 percent of résumés have inaccuracies, if not outright lies. In fact, candidates will often lie about their background. The most popular are fabrications about education. Often candidates will tell you about a college degree they never earned or a certificate they were never awarded. Sometimes they will tell you about a job they left because they were unhappy instead of the truth, which is that they were terminated.

How to Spot a Lie!

There is a way of finding out whether candidates (or anyone else) are telling the truth. When people are asked things that happened in the past, they will remember. When questions are asked about the future, people will create an answer. The problem is that when candidates are asked to recall past events, but then create answers, they are lying. Wouldn't it be helpful if you could find out a simple way of judging truthfulness during an interview? All within just a few seconds?

It's all involved in the way they move their eyes. Research from the University of California at Santa Cruz based on neurolinguistic programming (NLP) techniques discovered that people move their eyes in certain ways that indicate how they are thinking. When people move their eyes up, they are visualizing. When they will move their eyes to the side, they are hearing. When they look down, they are feeling.

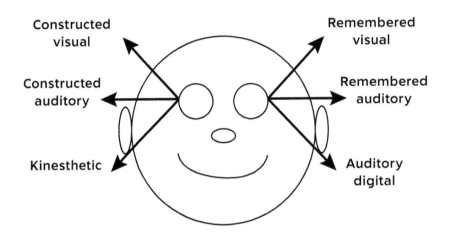

Richard Bandler and John Grinder, discoverers of NLP, found that eye movements correspond to words. For example, when people move their eyes up and visualize, they will use words like *see*, *picture*, *image*, *clear*, and *paint* (as in *paint a picture*). For example, they may say, "That's *clear* so far. I *see* your point." Or my favorite, "I *see* what you are saying."

You can test this on your own. Ask somebody to add two sets of two-digit numbers in their head. For example, "Please add 25 + 67." Watch where they move their eyes. It is nearly impossible to do addition in your head without making pictures. I remember a teacher in junior high school ask me to add three-digit numbers in my head. My eyes instantly moved up to the ceiling. Watching my eyes, she said, "Kerry, the answer is not on the ceiling." The problem is that none of us can add without making pictures.

When people move their eyes to the side, they tend to use sound-based words. These are *listen*, *hear*, *say*, *tone*, *ring*, and *resonate*. For example, my mother would say, "Don't take that *tone* with me, young man." On the phone I will often hear, "That *reso-*

nates with me." Or even, "That *rings a bell.*" My books sell so well on Audible.com partly because many people willing to listen to a book but not read it. This could be laziness, or it could be that they are more auditory learners: they tend to comprehend and remember ideas based on what they hear instead of what they read.

When people move their eyes down, they display feeling-based thoughts. These cognitions are reflected in words like *feel, strike,* and *grab.* For example, I frequently hear, "Do you *feel* me?" as a way of asking for understanding. Sometimes people will say, "That *strikes* me as a good idea." Or even, "That *grabs* me."

Bandler and Grinder noticed that when people move their eyes up to the right, they are imagining or thinking in the future. When they move their eyes up left, they are thinking in the past. For example, if you ask what my plans are tomorrow, my eyes will move up right. If you ask what I did yesterday, I will move my eyes up left.

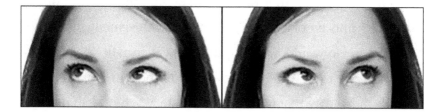

Here is how to spot a lie. If you read my résumé and ask me if I graduated with an MBA from Harvard and I look up to the right, I am constructing or creating an answer. This is a lie. If I look up left, I'm recalling where I went to college. That's the truth. The same is true for sounds. If you ask a candidate how they left their last job, and they look to the right, that's a fabrication. But if they look to the left, they are hearing past sounds reflective of why they left the former company. That's the truth.

The FBI and CIA both use this technique to find out whether informants are telling the truth. They can't take someone down to a police station for a lie detector test. They have to do preliminary interviews on the street. If an informant looks up to the right, agents know they are seeing a lie and will keep asking questions until they get the truth. This is exactly what you should do during an interview. If you see someone look up to the right, keep getting more detail until you get all the truth. Obviously, you can't accuse them of a lie. But you can be more elegant and gain more detail about the event.

A few years ago, I spoke at a mortgage conference in San Antonio, Texas. In the audience was a young man in his thirties who was a member of the Dallas Police Department. As a detective, he had the highest number of criminal confessions of anyone in Texas police history. After my speech, he said that he read one of my books and employed these same eye movement diagnostic techniques. He would always ask a suspect to talk about where they were and what they did at the time of the criminal event. He actually didn't care that much about the story as he did about their eyes. If he saw the suspect move their eyes up to the right or side right, he would dig deeper into the event details. Since very few people can remember details they lie about, the detective could usually catch them in a web of fabrications.

He also said very few people lie outright. Most people will instead accentuate certain words to deflect the question, for example, "*I* didn't say I was there." "I didn't say I was *there*." "I didn't *say*

I was there." All are accentuating different parts of the sentence. These are the kinds of cues the FBI is trained to notice during every interview. They don't really have time to do any more than quick interviews, so they have to be brilliant at reading people.

If you really want to hire great people, you have to be a great observer. You have to be a very good listener and pay attention to how things are said as well as what they say. You should also pay a great deal of attention to body language in order to read the candidate more effectively and make better behavioral predictions. You don't have to be a psychologist to be a good interviewer. You just have to pay attention. One of my favorite lines of all time is from the movie *Ghostbusters*, when Dan Akroyd said, "Listen. Do you smell something?"

Like any psychological rules, these have exceptions. You have to listen to the content and context of what you hear and see. If you ask where I was born, I will look up to the right and tell you Portland, Oregon. That is technically a lie, since I was born in Milwaukee, Oregon, a suburb of Portland. But to make it easier for the listener, I always say Portland. That is why you need to ask follow-up questions to get more accuracy.

When people ask what I do for living, I usually look up to the right and say, "business psychologist." A more accurate explanation of what I do is "speaker, author, and business coach." But often people don't know what that is, so I make it easier to understand by giving a more general answer.

When you are interviewing, you have to be aware of all this. You need to pay attention to where candidates move their eyes, the words they inflect, and whether they seem defensive or uncomfortable.

For example, if you see somebody look up to the right, ask them a few follow-up questions. If someone seems defensive or uncomfortable in discussing how they left their last employer, dig deeper and probe. If you notice discomfort or hostility in their answers, you have struck a chord. You may have caught them in a lie and boxed them in. Notice their stress level. Notice when they seem uncomfortable and edgy. Generally, people want to tell you the truth and how they feel. Communication is 82 percent emotion and nonverbal cues and 18 percent words. Pay 82 percent of your attention to their nonverbal cues and emotion and 18 percent to their words.

A great way to practice this is to watch late-night TV interview shows. You will get very good at spotting who's telling the truth and who's not.

How to Interview with Consistency: The Eleven Key Questions

Often managers are not good at hiring great people because they are subjective when they interview. In other words, no two candidates get the same question. At the end of the interview, the evaluator can only say whether they liked the candidate, not how candidates stack up against each other in any measured way. There is no standardized way of interviewing. There is no way of systematic scoring that can delete bias out of the selection.

Once I consulted for a company that had interviewed a new national sales manager. I asked the president what he thought. He mentioned how much he enjoyed the conversation, how enthusiastic the manager was, and the level of experience he displayed. I also asked the senior VP of marketing the same question. He said the total opposite. He didn't think the candidate had enough experience; he thought the recruit was lacking in enthusiasm and unfocused.

How could one candidate get such different evaluations from senior managers? The answer lies in how subjective they were in interviewing. Each manager listened and evaluated based on their own biases. Nothing was standardized.

Instead of hiring based on whether you like a candidate, use objective questions and evaluate the answers based on scores. Ask all of your candidates the same questions, and rate them according to how closely they adhere to the "correct" answers a perfect candidate would give. Simply invite the top three scorers back for a second interview. If you use this measured approach, you will make fewer emotional decisions that often end in lost time, money, momentum, and morale.

Here are the eleven questions you can ask during the interview that will make your interviews more measured and objective. Give each candidate a score based on the answers they give. Each question has total points for perfect answers.

1. WHY DID YOU LEAVE YOUR LAST JOB? (5 POINTS)

This question is based on the notion that the past is prologue. If someone left a job for a future greater opportunity, they are likely to pick their next one the same way. If someone left their past employer because of personality conflicts, they are likely to do the same in the future.

It's a little like the family with a U-Haul van full of furniture. They happened upon a gas station and asked the attendant about the next town. The worker instead asked what the town was like where they came from. The driver said it was full of wonderful people who are kind and generous. He hated to leave. But there were few jobs and he needed more opportunities to provide for his family. The attendant said he would find about the same thing up the road.

A few days later, the same situation happened. The next driver asked what the town was like, and the attendant responded with the same question: what was the town like where he came from? This driver reported a depressing place. The people were unfriendly, the schools were bad, and they were miserable there. The gas station worker said he would find about the same thing up the road.

Where someone came from and what they thought of their last job indicates what they will find in the future. People tend to find what they want. They rationalize and justify. Listen for this as you ask, "Why did you leave?"

If they left their last job for a greater opportunity, a challenge, or even to broaden their skills, they get a 5. If they instead talk about things they disliked about their last job or the people they couldn't get along with, the score is 0. If it's something in between those two extremes, give them a 1–4.

2. HOW DID YOU DECIDE TO SELECT YOUR LAST JOB? (5 POINTS)

A corollary to the concept that the past is prologue is asking how the candidate decided to select their last job. If someone picked it because of pay, more time off, or more flexible work hours, the score would be a 0. If they instead talk about more opportunity, greater challenge, and a chance to help the company become more successful, give them a 5. Alternatively, a 1–4 is an answer somewhere in the middle

While you're asking this question, a great follow-up is to ask what made them leave their last job, and why did they stay as long as they did. This is a great question to find out whether they have inertia or suffer from status quo. Often people will stay in a bad situation because they are afraid of change. This indicates someone who is willing to put up with a bad situation or not make a change because of low ambition.

I interviewed one candidate named Dave. He was in the company for ten years and told me candidly that he was unhappy the whole time. I asked him why he stayed so long. He admitted that he didn't try very hard to find a new position. Previously, we discussed the cost of keeping bad employees. If the people working for you right now are not the best you can find, they may be dragging down your business. The real cost to a business is not selecting the wrong people, it is keeping the wrong people too long.

3. THE "LET'S ASSUME" QUESTION (10 POINTS)

The "let's assume" technique is possibly the most important question you can ask. Not only will it allow you to discover what the candidate is looking for, but it will also show you how to keep them motivated. I love this question because you are putting the candidate three years in the future and asking what made them think this was the perfect position for them. What did they get? How much did they make? How much did they grow?

Here's the actual question: "Let's assume it's three years in the future. What happened that let you know that this was the perfect job and you had a great manager?"

Listen to their answer. You will almost always get three things the candidate wants. They will often talk about money, career growth, and communication. Many interviewers will hear the first part of the answer and jump in with, "We can do that." If you interrupt this question, you will not receive the benefit of what they want now and will keep them there later.

Quantify their response. Many candidates will give you emotional responses. They will say things like, "I just want to be happy." Or, "I want a position that is fulfilling." It's up to you to drill these emotions down to a much more tangible level. Your response should be, "What will make you happy?" Or, "What does 'fulfilling' mean to you?"

This is an amazing question for salespeople. One of my coaching clients asked a prospect, "Let's assume it's ten years in the future. What happened that let you know you had a perfect financial plan and we had a great relationship?" The prospect said, "I had enough money for retirement, my family was protected, and my financial advisor kept in touch." The financial advisor then asked, "How much money is enough?" The prospect said, "About $10,000 a month." He also asked, "What does 'Your family is protected' mean to you?" The prospect said, "If I die, I want my house to be paid off so my wife is protected." Lastly the financial advisor said, "What does 'keep in touch' mean?" The prospect said, "If I could hear from my advisor about every three months, that would make me happy."

The advisor then presented responses to the three things the prospect said he wanted. He moved a $3 million pension plan, earning fees of about $30,000 a year. This was mainly due to asking one question.

There is another huge benefit to the "let's assume" question. It allows you to motivate an employee by reverting back to the three goals you discovered during the hiring interview. If you can meet with your new employee every few months and ask about their progress towards the three goals you discovered in the interview, you are very likely to motivate people and keep them longer.

My client Matt runs a mortgage company in Utah. He lost two important staffers. One was a manager, the other, a loan processor. I asked why the manager left. Matt didn't know. This should never happen. We always want to keep good people and make sure they are motivated and happy. When unemployment is under 5 percent, the cost of replacing people is too much.

Recently, one of my coaching candidates, Joe, asked the "let's assume" question of a key staffer named Courtney. He was nervous that she would only last 3.6 years—the average for a millennial. He invested a lot of time and money developing Courtney. During lunch, he asked her the key question. Surprisingly, Courtney didn't know. Joe started throwing out possible options, like money, career growth, time off, and even enough assets to start a family. Courtney's creativity blossomed. The next week, Courtney thought a lot about what she wanted over the next three years and had some clear answers. Joe is now meeting with Courtney every three months and discussing her progress toward those goals.

Using the "let's assume" technique does not mean you are compromising performance for an employee's goals. But it does mean that you are keeping great people in addition to gaining their best performance.

If the candidate knows what they want in three years, a score of 10 is earned. If they have no idea what they want, give them a 0. If it's in between, score 1–9.

4. WHAT WAS YOUR BIGGEST SUCCESS? (10 POINTS)

Another great question to ask is a candidate's biggest and most memorable success. It is interesting to hear them define success as helping their last employer or as some achievement focused on themselves. Top producers will talk about a huge sale that benefited them and the company. They may also talk about starting a new division from scratch. Sometimes it the answer revolves around turning around a region that was failing.

Conversely, they may talk about personal success. It could be a lower score on their golf game, buying a new house, or even an association they belong to. While personal success can be remarkable, your goal is to hire someone who can help your company become more successful. If the candidate talks about personal successes more than career achievements, that may be a red flag.

My son-in-law is the president of a major biometric company. While it would make me very happy for him to report that his biggest success is as a father and husband, I wouldn't hire him for that. If I were interviewing him for a position, he would understand the context and talk about persuading his senior managers to develop a new division marketing to the federal government. His answer would include how he was able to make the division the most profitable in the company. Of course, hearing that answer would make you follow up with a question on how he did it.

If the candidate says their biggest success was helping a company shine, the score would be a 10. If their biggest success is personal or if they don't have a response, a 0 would be given. Or 1–9 if it's something in between.

5. WHAT WAS YOUR BIGGEST FAILURE? (10 POINTS)

Ask the candidate about their biggest failure. Some people like to call failures "setbacks" to be positive. Others tend to forget their failures and focus on the positives. But all of us fail. It's not failure that's important. It's the bounce back that's critical.

Legendary coach Vince Lombardi once said, "Success is never forever, and failure is never fatal." This question is important because you want to discover how the candidate recovered. You want to find out not how far they fell, but how high they bounced.

One of my clients interviewed a candidate recently. The candidate's past employer laid him off in a mass restructuring. The severance package was minimal and left the candidate with no income. He took a job as a regional manager in a division ranked last in the company. He turned the region around, making it number one in the company. Often, we will hear stories about a door opening after another closes. It's easy to say. But when a candidate experiences failure and then describes how they recovered, that is sheer courage. It also means they can overcome setbacks in your company as well.

If the candidate is able to tell you a story about a failure and subsequent bounce back, the score would be 10. If they don't have a story about failure, or remember the failure without recovery, you would give them a 0. Obviously, anything between is 1–9.

6. WHAT IS YOUR BIGGEST BEHAVIORAL WEAKNESS? (10 POINTS)

The purpose of this question is to find out whether the candidate is self-aware. Are they aware of personality and other work-related weaknesses? Do they know what to improve?

If you asked what my biggest weaknesses are, I would say lack of sufficient empathy, impatience, irritability, and perhaps work-aholism. My first marriage ended in divorce after seven years. While there were many issues, I'm sure that traveling five days a week sped its demise. An obvious follow-up question would be, "What am I now doing to become more empathetic and patient? How do I maintain a proportional work schedule?" The answer is that I am speaking now only about once a week. I make sure to talk to my kids in different states at least a few times a week. I strive to become a lot more grateful about everything. I also listen much more now instead of telling people what they should be doing.

Sometimes you will hear a candidate say things like, "Some people say I'm just too nice." Or, "I care about people too much. I am sometimes too trusting." These are nonresponses without candor. If the candidate knows their weaknesses and is able to tell you what they're doing to improve, you would rate the answer a 10. If they are not forthcoming with their weaknesses and don't have cogent strategies to improve, that would gain a 0. Anything in between would be 1–9.

7. EVER COLD-CALLED BEFORE? (20 POINTS)

One of my favorite questions is asking whether a candidate has cold-called. While you may not be hiring a telemarketer, it's useful to find out during the hiring process whether a candidate can put themselves into an uncomfortable position and still be successful.

One of the first things I asked my assistant Bethany was if she ever cold-called. She interpreted the question as whether I would put her on a telemarketing team and said no. I then followed up by asking if she ever had to offer something to someone she didn't know. She had experience fundraising for nonprofits and had called warm prospects for her last employer. She had cold-call experience but didn't even know it. I simply wanted to know whether she would freeze up if I put her in a position where she had to persuade people she did not know.

Cold-calling experience gets a 20. If they have been insulated from talking to and/or persuading people they don't know, they would get a 0. Anything in between would be 1–19.

8. WHAT ARE YOUR GOALS? WHAT IS YOUR PLAN TO HIT THEM? (5 POINTS)

This is one of my favorite questions, but only about 18 percent of candidates will be able to answer it. In fact, the late, great motivational speaker Zig Ziglar once said, "Only 2 percent of a Yale University graduating class had goals. Yet they achieved more than the other 98 percent over their lifetime." Whether this statistic was exaggerated or true, people with goals always achieve more. And people who have plans to achieve goals and implement them are the often the real superstars you are looking for.

One of my coaching clients currently sells healthcare plans by telephone in New Jersey. He read one of my books and called me to help him hit his goals. Only twenty-six years old, he was completely focused. He knew the income level he wanted over the next three years. He wanted to learn how to get there. He implemented everything we talked about and was always prepared. I can say that is true of only 25 percent of the people I coach. Although I require my coaching clients to study five minutes every day and implement the skills we talk about, Danny is one of the very few who actually did it. His diligence showed. He was on track to increase sales by at least 50 percent that year. These are the types of people you and I both want to hire.

If a candidate knows what their goals are, has a plan to hit them, give them a 5 on the points scale. If they don't know, give them a 1. Anything in between is 1–4.

9. WHO WAS YOUR OR YOUR COMPANY'S LONGEST CLIENT? WHY DID THEY STAY WITH YOU? (5 POINTS)

This question is about client relationships. It reflects both the company's commitment to customers as well as the employee's dedication to relationships.

Many of my coaching clients will tell me that their clients are some of their best friends. They play golf with them, go to dinner, and talk frequently. Their clients stay for years and even a lifetime. Many will make a sale and never talk to the client again. During my speeches over forty years, I constantly remind audiences that 89 percent of what clients value most are relationships, not price.

I recommend attendees call their own clients every three months. Those that do always see 30 percent increases in sales.

You can test this out. The next time a prospect is about to buy, tell them, "Once you sign the contract, it will be the last time I ever talk to you." If you sense the prospect is hesitant, you may understand this point. I know exactly why my coaching clients stay with me for so many years. First, I keep them accountable to their business plan. I make sure their activity is consistent. Second, I give them new skills on a weekly basis to make their job easier. Adhering to a weekly business activity goal is like peddling a bicycle. Applying skills is steering it.

If the candidate can name their most long-standing client or customer and knows why they stayed, a 5 is earned. If they can't or don't know how they retained the client, give them a 0. Or a 1–4, depending on the answer.

10. WHY DO YOU WANT THIS JOB? (5 POINTS)

This is probably the most common question any interviewer will ask. But if asked the right way, you may get more than a rhetorical response. Some candidates may just throw darts at a job board to find the best opportunity. Others really want to work for your company. We are trying to find out whether the candidate considers your opportunity a job or a way to grow and help your company at the same time.

Candidates who talk about the opportunity to work with you in your company get a 5. If the recruit doesn't know or seems disingenuous, give them a 0. Or 1–4 for anything in between.

11. HOW WOULD YOU SELL ME THIS PEN? (35 POINTS)

One of the fun questions is to ask the candidate to sell you a pencil or pen. This gets 35 points. Often my coaching clients ask me why they should do this with an administrative assistant instead of just with potential salespeople. And why so many points?

Fifteen years ago, I worked as a consultant for Beverley Healthcare. They were trying to develop a new division selling managed care. They had assisted-living hospitals all across America. They were trying to gain more revenue with patients that had acute needs for managed care. They wanted to fill hospitals on a short-term basis. I visited twenty cities within three months. Every regional manager had an excuse for lacking sales. They ranged from poor economic conditions, difficulty working with insurance companies, and even their own support staff. Finally in Minneapolis, I asked a regional director to sell me a pen.

The father of modern-day sales is J. Douglas Edwards. He was on *The Mike Douglas Show* twenty years before Oprah became the queen of daytime television. During the last ten-minute block, J. Douglas was introduced as the best salesperson on earth. Mike said, "Sell me this ashtray." J. Douglas asked Mike what he liked best about the ashtray. Mike said the green color; it was his favorite. J. Douglas then asked what else he liked. Mike said the heft of the ashtray, because it was a good paperweight. During commercials, they would fire up the swamp coolers, blowing his interview notes around. The ashtray was heavy enough to keep them organized. He finally liked the channels on top of the ashtray to put his cigarettes on. Mike was a chain smoker and didn't want the cigarettes to fall off, burning the studio down. Finally, J. Douglas asked, "How much, Mike, would you pay for the ashtray? "Mike said, "$5." J. Douglas finally replied, "Sold; it's yours."

After the Minneapolis manager sold me the pencil, I told him the J. Douglas Edwards ashtray story and asked him to sell me the pen again. The manager tried to sell me the exact features he did a few minutes ago, learning nothing from the story. I knew immediately that nobody in the company was listening to their prospects and customers. They all were all trying to sell managed care without paying attention to needs. They didn't have effective sales skills. Also, the manager in Minneapolis wasn't coachable.

Ask your candidates to sell you a pen or pencil, and then tell them the J. Douglas Edwards story and ask them to sell it again. If they first ask you what you like about the pen and then sell you those features, you have a candidate who is coachable and can learn. If they sell the pen the same way, you have somebody that will be tough to coach and difficult to develop. The coachable candidates get 35 points. The noncoachable ones get 0 or a number in between.

I realize that these are all generic questions that may not apply to the position you're interviewing for. Feel free to change any of them, or the scores, to make them more relevant. The most important thing is to make the questions consistent for all candidates. That'll make the selection process a lot easier and more predictable.

As you meet with candidates, make sure that every interviewee gets the same questions. If you can standardize your scores, you are likely to be more objective and able to pick good people instead of subjectively selecting candidates based on your emotions. If you ask a candidate to interview with you and somebody else, compare scores with your colleague. It'll give you a framework for evaluating people that is better than merely whether you like or dislike them.

Emotional Intelligence

In any interview, the way you ask is as important as the questions. Only journalists and police officers interrogate from a sheet of paper. The rest of us need to put empathy and context into why we are asking questions. Also, to get the response we're hoping for.

For example, using the "let's assume" technique, you would ask the textbook question: "Let's assume it's three years in the future. How would you know you had a perfect job and a great relationship with your supervisor?"

A much better way to ask the question would be, "I would love to find out more about what your expectations are. If we end up working together, what it would take to motivate you to stay with us? Let's assume it's three years in the future. What happened that let you know it was a perfect job and you had a great relationship with your supervisor?" Asking a question with context and intent will generate better responses than just reading the question and filling in a box. Great interviewers listen for answers and follow up appropriately. Bad interviewers ask questions and then move on.

One of the hardest skills to teach my coaching clients is listening. An even more difficult skill is to listen and ask follow-up questions. A client may ask questions of a prospect and hear, "I will think about it," or "Let me think it over." These are both stalls. Often they are reflexive, unthinking responses. Yet most interviewers accept the response at face value, lacking the skill to ask follow-up questions. They need a clarification response like, "I know this is a lot to think about. What is your biggest concern right now?" Or, "I understand. What is your biggest worry about this?"

When my wife responds with "Fine," I don't just accept the answer and walk away. "Fine" usually means anything but. As I ask a follow-up question, I learn she is irritated, upset, or both. Asking the right follow-up questions usually keeps me out of the penalty box.

This is a good example of listening for intent, context, and content as you ask the eleven key questions. No professional interviewer, whether a trial lawyer, police detective, psychologist, or any other professional communicator, should ever let responses stand on their own. You are picking somebody who could substantially help build your company or who could be a complete headache. Which one you get may depend on how well you can probe and ask questions. The better you listen for the meaning of a response, the more you will learn about the candidate.

Interview Etiquette

When there is a high unemployment rate, interviewers can pick and choose candidates from a very large pool. Interviewer behavior makes less of a difference. But when unemployment is low, it's critical that you treat the applicant not only with respect but also etiquette.

Employers are taking twice as long to hire as they did a decade ago. Many employers in the past have ghosted (not responded) applicants instead of being direct and responsive. Many candidates have interviewed but fail to get any follow-up from the employer. Many others say employers are dismissive of applications and even disrespectful during interviews. That may have been more tolerated in a high unemployment environment, but not when the labor market is tight.

In a low unemployment market, interview etiquette is critical. The behavior employers could get away with ten years ago does not work today. In one study by Future Workplace and Career Arc, 60 percent of job seekers say being treated badly would make them less likely to buy the company's products, let alone consider employment. While 91 percent of employers say that the candidate's experience can affect their decision to should join a firm, only 26 percent of employers measure how the candidate feels after the interview.

Many candidates spend a lot of time preparing for an interview. They may research the company, products, sales, and even financials. Yet candidates often receive no follow-up from the interviewers, whether it's a phone call or even an email.

It's understandable that employers would rather not call a candidate with bad news. They would rather just ignore the situation than engage in an awkward conversation. In my career, I've been ghosted by companies in booking myself as a speaker. I may have a telephone interview with a key executive that I thought went well, but when I tried to follow up, there was no response.

The Up-Front Close

The answer to all this is the *up-front close*. The up-front close is a way to get both the employer and the candidate to say yes or no, but not maybe. I teach my coaching clients to always start a presentation by asking prospects to be totally honest and direct. The biggest problem in sales is the stall. The prospect or client says, "Let me think about it." The salesperson takes that seriously and then follows up with five or six phone calls. When the client finally answers the phone, they say, "I meant to call you. We decided not to do this." It's likely that the client never intended to make a purchase in the first place. If that's true, wouldn't a no be better than a stall?

Here's a way to use the up-front close during an interview. "Before we start, I want to let you know that if we both agree this is the right position for you, I hope you'll say yes. If for any reason you decide that this is the not the right career path, I hope you'll say no. But what I'd rather you not do is say, 'Let me go think about it,' or 'I will get back to you,' because that tells me you don't have enough information to make a decision. You will not hurt my feelings by saying no. Is that OK with you?"

Since many candidates are too afraid to say no, they need permission to be honest and candid. As you ask them to be candid, let them know it will be reciprocated. You will be direct with them as well.

I use the up-front close in my practice daily. Before the evaluation questions on an initial coaching candidate call, I will always start the presentation with the up-front close. If I'm trying to book myself as a speaker and have a conference call with decision makers, I will religiously use the up-front close. It is never awkward. But it is direct enough that people will usually say, "Of course."

A few years ago, a coaching client told me why he agreed to coaching. I didn't give him an option to say maybe. He admitted procrastinating about nearly everything in his life. He usually avoided decisions, often landing in trouble. But since I would not allow a stall, he didn't want to say no. I laughed and said, "At least you made a decision." The up-front close will save you time and aggravation if both you and the candidate can be candid, direct, and honest.

Here are a few things to keep in mind during any interview:
1. Make sure your job posting accurately describes the position.
2. Respond to candidates' résumés as soon as they are received.
3. Keep candidates informed about where they stand.
4. Let candidates know immediately if the job or the process changes during the middle of a search.
5. Leave all applicants with a positive image of your company.

When Candidates Are Overqualified

Have you ever interviewed an overqualified candidate? Have you ever spoken to someone with too much experience or too much education? Many candidates wrongly assume a star-studded résumé is a surefire path to a great job. But according to a study at Carnegie Mellon University, being too qualified or having too much experience may not be attractive to employers. Organizational psychology researchers found that managers often have biases toward people who seem too good for a job.

Researcher Dr. Oliver Hahl tested managers' willingness to make an offer to two candidates for a corporate finance job. Both had stellar résumés. One had experience heading a ten-person team financing $1.5 billion in transactions, while the other headed a much smaller team doing deals about one tenth the size of the other's. The hiring managers were much more likely to make an offer to the candidate with the less impressive record than to the $1.5 billion superstar. The managers' bias was that the candidate with the stellar résumé would not be as motivated or committed to the company as the less experienced candidate. The bias was more about motivation and job longevity than performance. The research also showed that supervisors may be threatened by the superstar's lack of willingness to take direction.

Often a candidate is labeled *overqualified* as a euphemism for *too old*, but since employers can't discriminate on age, the *overqualified* label takes its place. But younger applicants can also be labeled wrongly. In one study evaluating candidates with MBAs, there was bias against Ivy League degrees and toward second-tier business school graduates. Candidates from the less well-known MBA schools with straight A's and a record of accomplishment were thought to be more motivated and scrappier. The top-tier MBA school graduates were perceived as prima donnas or more self-absorbed. They were thought less willing to get along with coworkers.

I wrote previously that Abraham Lincoln's cabinet in the nineteenth century was said to contain rivals. In fact, CEOs need advisors who don't necessarily agree with their decisions and can point out problems. Yet interviewers tend to pick people who can get along with others instead of select those who push back with better ideas. They'd rather hire people who can cooperate.

One candidate with a top-tier résumé no longer wanted the stress of senior management. After taking time off to raise a child, she wanted a job with less stress and more flexibility. Many players saw her as overqualified and therefore unacceptable.

My brother Kevin interviewed as a national sales manager with a turf company producing artificial grass. At fifty-seven years old, he had run his own video training company for nearly thirty years. He led a team of more than ten salespeople and demanded consistent performance. The turf company president thought Kevin was overqualified. This could have been age discrimination. But Kevin could have easily doubled the company's sales within only a year. Since my brother was so qualified, the president may have felt threatened or uncomfortable. But he did admit that he thought Kevin would not stay in the job or feel motivated to work long hours.

The answer to overqualification problems is to listen to why the candidate wants the job. Listen for their motivation and whether their reasoning makes sense. Perhaps they want a lifestyle change. Perhaps they have decided to try a new career path. A few of my friends are lawyers who decided in midcareer to pursue a nonlegal path.

Earlier we spoke about emotional intelligence. Instead of listening to a candidate tell you the job is right for them, ask why. Dig deeper into their motivation for taking a job that, on the surface, would not appear to suit them. If they don't have a compelling reason, they may truly be overqualified.

When a New Hire Doesn't Show

In a high unemployment environment, candidates are excited about almost any opportunity. In a low unemployment environment, several offers may compete with yours. Candidates may be juggling multiple job offers. If that happens, they may take the path of least resistance and not communicate at all. In one case, a candidate accepted a job offer but didn't show up on the first day. The manager called the search firm and asked for help. The headhunter called the new hire's house. A man answered the telephone who claimed to be the uncle and said his nephew had passed away. The search firm later discovered that he was actually alive but didn't want to face the manager with bad news.

According to a recent survey by Robert Half Associates, 25 percent of new hires say they've backed out after accepting a new job. While job seekers of any age may ghost or back out of a new job, it's most common among those with two to six years' experience in the workforce. One headhunter explained that this is the generation that breaks up romances with text messages. It's not hard to imagine they would do the same with a job.

Sometimes the candidate gets a better offer from a current employer. Other times a competitor increases a bid. It always seems as if a grenade is thrown into the mix. Many years ago, I hired an assistant who seemed very excited about the opportunity. During the interview, she asked for two weeks for a family vacation. I was thrilled and agreed to her request since I received so many glowing recommendations from past employers. After two weeks passed, she didn't show up for her first day. I called and heard she accepted another job a week earlier. She could have let me know and saved a week searching for another person.

Here are a couple of tips to make sure your next hire doesn't ghost you.

1. Ask the candidate for their timeline in selecting a new job.
2. Ask the candidate what other positions they are evaluating.
3. Always do the up-front close during the interview.
4. Do a trial close at the end of the interview. Ask the candidate if they think the opportunity is right from what they have heard so far.
5. Always have a backup plan. Keep interviewing for a second person in case the first choice doesn't work out. Be prepared for a no-show. Although this is less likely to happen with those possessing more experience and age, nobody wants to start the search process again.

If you are hiring administrative staff, you need to also evaluate fundamental skills. Basic communication and math skills should also be tested. One of my coaching clients hired an assistant. Before gaining the skills from this book, she hired based only on emotion. She quickly realized the assistant could not even do simple math. In addition, the assistant consistently misspelled words in emails to clients. The manager had to proofread and check nearly everything the assistant did. Because of the extra work, it was worse than having no assistant at all.

Here are 2 basic skill checks you should use:

1. Ask them to solve a simple eighth-grade word problem. For example:

   "Jill went to the store with $10. She had to buy milk for $2.50 and a newspaper for $1 and get $5 worth of gas. She took the milk back for a refund because it was spoiled. How much is she left with?" The answer is $10 – $2.50 – $1 – $5 = $1.50 + $2.50 for the milk refund = $4. You will be shocked how many candidates won't get that answer.

2. Dictate a paragraph and ask the candidate to write it out in longhand. Check for spelling, grammar, and whether you can actually read their writing. This will be critical: you don't want to get handwritten messages with unreadable spelling errors.

   Both of these skill checks are crucial for administrative candidates. You obviously don't need this when hiring supervisory or expert staff. But you could save yourself a lot of grief if you can find out their basic skill set in the beginning.

Hiring Biases

How important are good looks in your hiring decision? Five percent? Ten percent? How about 70 percent?

According to most personality evaluation research, 70 percent of why you pick people is based on their appearance. Most of this is due to the halo effect. If someone is good-looking, we think of them as smart, honest, and hard-working. In fact, most criminal prosecutors know it's harder to convict a good-looking person than someone less attractive.

Here's another question: "Can a woman be too pretty to thought of as a good candidate?"

In a University of Minnesota research study, pictures of four people were evaluated. They were all said to be very successful. One was of a good-looking man. Another was of a less attractive man. There were also photos of a very attractive woman and a less attractive female. Research participants were all asked the reason for their success.

The good-looking man was judged successful because of his hard work, intelligence, and ethics: the typical halo effect. The less attractive man was deemed successful because he was the boss's son and/or had connections. The pretty woman was deemed successful because she was an attractive image for the company, good at PR, and a good client entertainer. The less attractive woman was reported to be successful for the same reasons as the attractive man: she was hard-working, well-educated, and motivated. The common theme between the good-looking man and the less attractive woman was masculinity. The more masculine people appear, the better candidates they seem to be.

This is important when you make judgments about candidates. An attractive woman may have skills unrelated to her looks. The same may be true for an unattractive man. The lesson here is to wait at least thirty minutes before you make an evaluation. The image of a candidate will disappear as you see the whole person.

There are exceptions. Entertainers may need to be attractive first. A TV host will need some level of attraction. A friend told me he is amazed at how many beautiful women are on Fox News. Of course: they are selected for appearance, at least to some degree.

Attractiveness has to do with the whole package. In the popular movie *Basic*, John Travolta was investigating a murder in Panama. As he arrived from the US, he asked the local military investigator if the suspect was cute. She seemed insulted at the question. He clarified by saying, "Is he attractive? It has nothing to do with looks. Does he make you think he is attractive by the way he talks, carries himself, and engages you in conversation?" This is the real meaning of attractiveness, and not many candidates have it.

The application here is for a man to dress more nicely and for a woman to dress in a more subdued fashion. The more a candidate can take away initial biases, the more smoothly the interview can go.

Hire for Energy and Enthusiasm?

Do you ever try to hire energetic and enthusiastic people? Have you ever been around someone so enthusiastic that they got on your nerves? The central characteristic should be versatility. How well do they adapt to others? The way to test this is with multiple interviews. Just because you like the candidate doesn't mean others will. As a rule of thumb, have the candidate interview at least one other person using the eleven key questions. You can compare scores to come to a better selection.

The First Impression

How quickly during an interview are you likely to make an emotional decision about a candidate? One hour? Two hours? How about four minutes? According to Los Angeles psychiatrist Leonard Zunin, author of *Contact: The First Four Minutes,* we make more than 93 percent of our lasting impressions about people in the first four minutes. This means your chance of finding somebody good based on a four-minute evaluation is zero. One rule of thumb in interviewing is to avoid making any judgments about people until after the first thirty minutes. I know this is extremely difficult. But if you wait to make any judgment about candidates for at least thirty minutes, you may find your initial biases were mistaken. If you can live by this rule, you may find superstars.

One of my clients interviewed candidates for a sales job. One prospect who had great energy was substantially obese. My client was immediately turned off. But then he remembered my thirty-minute rule. After the first four minutes of the interview, he learned the candidate had doubled his last employer's sales within six months.

Here's another question: A candidate has interviewed twice with different people. You've evaluated based on energy and past performance. You've waited thirty minutes without making a decision. You've asked the eleven key questions, and your candidate scored best among all the others. Do you make an offer? Not unless you want to make another critically bad hiring decision.

Hire slow, fire fast. Easy to hear, tough to implement. You also may have been so desperate to find someone that you made an offer to the first person who looked good. I'll also bet by the time you decided to fire a bad employee, it was six months later than they should have terminated. I have never heard any of my clients say they terminated an employee at exactly the right time. It always should have been months or even years earlier. I realize there are no perfect people out there. But you shouldn't tolerate people who can't do the job. Don't rationalize poor performance. Fire fast. Get rid of poor performers.

Checking with Past Employers

I have frequently mentioned that the past is prologue. How people behave in the past indicates how they will act in the future. I've also mentioned that your chances of getting the right person from an interview alone are very poor, because candidates are more experienced in interviewing than you. Also, most employers believe the initial façade that candidates portray. They are unlikely to find out who the real person is. Many interviewers choose to believe what candidates want to show you.

My daughter Caroline applied for an apartment lease in San Diego. The landlord called three of the references Caroline listed. One was me. The landlord started the conversation by telling me where the apartment was and how much the rent was. He then asked me how well I knew Caroline. I admitted that I was her father and was frankly surprised that he called me for a reference; I am probably the most biased person he could have called. It's surprising that employers actually call references who are friends and colleagues of the applicant. Instead, we need to call those who can tell us frankly about the candidate's past performance and behavior.

One great way of finding out who the candidate really is behind the façade to check with past employers. Ask the candidate for the names and contact information of the past two supervisors, and call them. But avoid talking to the HR manager if you can. The HR person is trained to tell you when the candidate was employed and the position they held, but nothing about their performance. Even savvy HR professionals don't know what they can and can't say. Because of this, they tell you almost nothing.

Many years ago, I brought a real estate partnership prospectus to my CPA. He reviewed it for a week, told me about its myriad problems, and said I should stay away from it. I brought another, eliciting the same response. Frustrated, I brought the third and final prospectus, only to hear how much the CPA disliked that one as well. Finally, I asked the CPA what kind of real estate partnership he did like. He admitted that he would recommend none, since if any blew up, I would blame him. After spending $4,500 in partnership review fees, I found that I had wasted it all. I thought my CPA would recommend one if it was good. The same is true with HR directors. They will neither tell you the good nor the bad, only that the person worked there, along with the beginning and ending dates.

Supervisors are different than the HR folks. They are like you. They know the importance and difficulty of finding good people. They also have a sense of legal consequences. Some may resist telling you anything bad about an applicant, but they can be encouraged. If you want to hire somebody good, don't depend on your own judgment. You have to get information from a past employer. It's important that you talk to the direct supervisor. If the manager is once removed from your applicant, you won't learn much about their strengths and weaknesses. But the supervisor knows.

The supervisor also has to hire and knows how difficult that task can be. They're much more likely to be honest with you about the candidate. Tell the supervisor about the job duties you require and ask them whether the candidate has the skills and mindset to be successful. Most of the time, the supervisor will be candid.

Sometimes the supervisor won't talk about the applicant. Perhaps they were warned they could be sued. Perhaps the applicant was terminated, and the supervisor was warned not to discuss it. A few years ago, my favorite golf teacher was fired from our country club. One day I showed up for a lesson and asked about him. The head pro would only say my teacher was gone and probably won't come back. I sarcastically said, "Is he on vacation? Is he sick? Is he in prison?" They head pro only said, "I can't talk about him. Most employees in his position would not be rehired." That's all I could get. I found out later that my teacher was taking tips without reporting them to the teaching staff. If that was an infraction, I was guilty, since my tips were always in cash. But why the mystery for such a small infraction? Once I discovered the reason after a few weeks of investigating, I tracked him down at another club and resumed lessons.

Getting the Truth from Reluctant Supervisors

In case you encounter a reticent supervisor, here are some suggestions. Supervisors really want to be candid, but think they can't. You might want to try these questions: "I know you can't talk about the candidate. But if you could, what would you say?" This is one of my favorite lines. It will cause the supervisor to laugh and open up. I did this with one supervisor a few years ago. He was tight-lipped and wouldn't respond. I used this line, and he chuckled. He said, "You sound like my life insurance agent. He always gets me to talk about how I really feel." He was candid and opened up. He said the candidate was a great hire and that he was sorry to lose him.

If they still don't want to talk, use this line. "We have a policy in our company to always get a recommendation, good or bad, from past supervisors. Otherwise, we can't hire the candidate. It would be a shame if I couldn't make an offer because we can't get an evaluation." If the supervisor is still silent, they are trying to avoid a bad report. This is a red flag that your candidate would be a bad hire.

Obviously, you want to ask the supervisor why the candidate left. If they were terminated, find out why. That is why it's always a good idea to talk to the past two employers instead of just one. But if they left on good terms, use my favorite question to past supervisors, "Would you hire them again if you got the chance?" I am always looking for great people to hire in the future. If the employer says anything except that they would love to hire the candidate again if a position opens up, don't hire. That could be another red flag.

You might be thinking that because somebody failed at their last job, it doesn't mean they can't be successful at yours. That could be true. But it's a risky decision. You don't want to make a hiring decision based on just your gut. Use your head. Elsewhere in this book I've discussed how keeping a bad hire is worse than making a hiring mistake in the first place. It's really not that you hired a bad candidate but that you kept them. Your first and best chance at selecting somebody good is getting the truth from a past employer.

The Past Is Prologue

Can people really change? Again, as I've emphasized, the answer is no. Who we are at the core, including our ethics, manners, and personality, doesn't change. We can learn, but we can't change who we are except in the most unique of circumstances. How a candidate performed in their last job will probably predict how they will perform in yours.

Many years ago, I owned a video training company with my brother Kevin. These videos were sold by a telemarketing team supervised. One of the telemarketers was a stellar performer at first. But after two weeks, Kevin fired him. A month later, Brian, a famous motivational speaker and a friend of mine, called to say he was about to hire the telemarketer and wanted a recommendation. I told my friend the salesman was a drug addict, stole from us, and was the worst hire we ever made. Brian unbelievably said, "At our company, we transform people from who they are to what they can be." I smiled on the telephone and said, "Good luck."

At a conference a month later, I saw Brian and asked about how the telemarketer was doing. Brian said he started out well. But after three days, he asked Brian if he could have a $3,500 advance so he could buy a car. He had to take the bus to work, and it took him an hour each way. With a car, he could come in an hour earlier and make more sales. Brian fell for this and gave the guy the $3,500.

After three days the marketer didn't show up for work. After two more weeks and ten voice mail messages, Brian finally got through to him. He said, "I realize you are not coming back to work. But can you at least return the $3,500?" The drug addict said, "If you wanted the $3,500 back, you should not have given it to me in the first place." Can people change? Sometimes. But don't bet your hiring decisions on it.

Job Testing

Many recruiters are using personality testing more and more. But do tests really predict behavior? Can they help you select the right person? Are they biased? Will they produce false positives or tell you yes when your gut tells you no?

Many employers hope to take the risk out of selection by testing. But any assessment should merely serve as a backup to your own decisions. Big corporations have used employment testing for decades. Now even smaller companies can make better decisions by using off-the-shelf tests.

The life insurance industry has used sales performance tests for decades produced by the Life Insurance Marketing Research Association (LIMRA). It is a standard in the industry. This personality profile has become so popular that many branch managers are prohibited from selecting a candidate with a bad LIMRA score. It measures everything from extraversion to how many friends they have, as well as the skills that have produced success in the past and predict the chances for success in the future. It works except when it doesn't. Branch managers have become so dependent on this test they sometimes disqualify candidates with bad test scores, going against their own gut.

Any testing should be a backup, not a determinant. The most important indicators of success in the future are those that occurred in the past. That's why talking to past supervisors is critical. In a perfect world, testing will give you strengths, weaknesses, and areas to be improved. Testing will let you know about the candidate's training needs as well as guiding your supervision. But a test should not be definitive.

One benefit of good testing is whether the candidate is a cultural fit. Hiring a maverick into a team of technical contributors would create friction. One popular test, the Myers-Briggs Type Indicator, groups people into sixteen different types. It separates the introverts from extraverts and gives you an idea of who the logically minded are and who are the emotionally driven. This is important for learning what you can expect from a candidate and how they may react in certain situations.

For example, you may not learn much about whether a candidate will complete a task, but you may learn a lot about how stressed they get when they are pressured by deadlines. You may also learn how well they collaborate on a team.

Many companies are now using personality tests to set baseline behaviors with their own employees. For example, a sales organization may test their top-tier salespeople. They may discover, for example, that the best producers are not as affected by rejection as the lower achieving group. They may also discover that top producers have more emotional intelligence (EQ) than those who are not as successful.

Some organizations employ TTI testing services. Others use the DiSC model to evaluate candidates. These assessments will at minimum give you more insight into the person you are interviewing.

Benchmarking

The best way to use any test is to ask those already working for you to take the test themselves. Any test can give you basic tendencies of a candidate. But perhaps the position you are hiring for needs a special combination of skills and talents. For example, a financial wholesaler needs not only sales skills but also the ability to speak in front of many different audiences. An executive assistant may need to accompany the boss on trips and keep the schedule organized as well as being able to supervise home office staff.

Benchmarking the job is the best way to inventory the skills and abilities you will need to select for. No test will give you a completely accurate view of the person capabilities and the emotional intelligence to use them. But benchmarking your successful producers will get close. Along with your expert interviewing skills, you will give your self and the candidate a good chance of success.

Benchmarking can be done with your own staff or subject experts. For example, you may be tempted to sample the top performer in your company, but your top employee may be an underachiever compared to others in your industry. To prevent this kind of bias, you may want to call your local industry trade group or association if they have any test results from other members.

For example, the top performers in your industry may be college-educated, call on ten prospects every day, and possess an extraverted personality. They may also be oriented toward the big picture and avoid detail, suggesting the need for an administrative assistant.

The important point here is to find out who top performers are and what they do. Then select for those behaviors. If you can use a template, you job of selecting good people will be much easier.

In my forty years of experience, I have seen many top sales professionals fail and succeed, but the best have possessed certain commonalities. Top sales producer traits to select for are:

1. GOAL FOCUS.

They will do anything to hit a goal. They will work nights and weekends and move mountains to hit an objective. They may need coaching in developing skills, but they relish the chance to improve.

2. THEY QUICKLY BOUNCE BACK FROM REJECTION.

The biggest producers don't avoid rejection. While they don't look for it, they think of rejection as just a number. They know ten rejections may be in store before they get a yes.

3. THEY HAVE HIGH LEVELS OF EMOTIONAL INTELLIGENCE.

They are able to read people effectively. They listen more than they talk. They don't pitch. They listen for opportunities and then suggest solutions to clients' needs.

4. THEY ARE VERY COACHABLE.

They look for ways to do things better. They are always looking for skills or tools that can help make more money. They are not just marking time; they are keen on improving.

5. THEY HAVE A RESULTS-FOCUSED MINDSET.

I wrote a book in 2018 entitled *New Mindset, New Results*. I explained both the *fixed* and *growth* mindsets. Fixed-mindset people are stuck. When presented with new ideas, they revert back to what they already know. They discount any new techniques, clawing back to the same things they had been doing. When presented with setbacks, they make excuses or blame other people. They often think of themselves as better than others and are unwilling to improve.

Those with a growth mindset continue to learn. They look at setbacks as stepping-stones to doing things better the next time. When they listen to other people, they strive to gain something they can use instead of dismissing the conversation. They look at risk as an opportunity to get better instead of as a possible loss.

The *results-focused mindset* is the main subject of my book. These professionals realize that first they need to set a goal, then change their mindset to achieve it. This could involve increasing work hours, taking a training course, or reorganizing a team. During the research for this book, I discovered that most people will dismiss an opportunity because it requires too much change. But results-focused people will critically assess everything they have to do to achieve the goal and determine whether they are willing to put in the effort.

During our first coaching session, I tell every new client that there are no unrealistic goals. The only question is whether the client can commit to an activity plan and be disciplined enough to follow it. A good example of the results-focused mindset is a special operations mission in the military. The task is assigned to the commander, who then creates a plan to accomplish it. It could take a larger team, more specialized skills, or even a longer planning process. But the mission is the mission. It may require a new mindset to accomplish, but it is up to the commander to teach new skills or else inform the leader that task can't be completed with the current skill set.

While we would love to have every candidate possess a results-focused mindset, this trait is especially important in sales. Although there is no assessment that can discover a results-focused mindset, you can listen for cues to determine if the candidate has a growth or fixed mindset. If the candidate gives you excuses, they may have more of a fixed mindset. If the candidate talks about how they overcame obstacles or what they learned from setbacks, they may possess a growth-focused mindset. But if the candidate discussed what they learned in order to accomplish a goal—for example, achieving a promotion and getting an MBA in the process—they have a results-focused mindset.

Other Tests That May Help

Here are some popular tests you can use. While no test is definitive, these can help you make better decisions.

JOB KNOWLEDGE TESTS

These tests may illuminate a candidate's technical or expertise in a given field. For example, accountants may be given a test reviewing their skills. Coders may be given a test to reveal their computer language skills and accuracy.

There is a famous scene in the movie *The Social Network* where Facebook founder Mark Zuckerberg tests six college students on their computer coding skills late at night. They are all required to drink alcohol at regular intervals to the cheers of a crowd of fellow students. Zuckerberg only selected one of the six who could code accurately with no sleep and while drunk. This may not be a test you would use, but it is a humorous example of testing for technical expertise.

INTEGRITY TESTS

One of most common preemployment tests are focused on honesty, ethics, and reliability. There are both overt and covert forms of integrity tests. Some ask the candidate directly if they have ever stolen anything. More overt ways of asking this question are, "Have you ever received something that was stolen?" Or, "Have you ever received something that was not yours?"

More sophisticated personality tests will ask about ethics in multiple ways. Good integrity tests tend to be unbiased. There is no measurable difference between age, race, or culture when it comes to morality. There is no culture where stealing is condoned.

In my graduate MBA program, an ethics course was required of all students. In the beginning, all of us knew right from wrong.

But there are many shades of gray. During the final exam, an essay question was posed about doing business in South America. The scenario was this: "The government requires bribes, and every competitor is paying. But it is against US law to engage in that activity. There is a special corporate fund set up for emergencies that is nonreportable to US headquarters. If there is a choice between failing to complete the task in the South American country or making money for the company using bribes, what should the country manager do?"

Most of us knew deep down it is wrong to pay bribes. All my graduate student colleagues also knew that failing to pay would create failure for the foreign unit of our imaginary company. The right answer, according to the professor, was to report the bribery culture to the US headquarters and ask for reassignment.

While this case study presented an ethical dilemma, it's better to find out what a candidate might do during preemployment testing. Depending on the position, an ethical mistake may create legal disaster for a company that costs millions in penalties.

COGNITIVE ABILITY TESTS

These kinds of tests tend to be good predictors of job performance. Some recruiters even believe they are better predictors than interviews or the candidate's experience. Tests like the General Aptitude Test (GAT) can measure logical, verbal, and numerical reasoning.

As with most tests, there may be racial and ethnic differences creating varying results. When my coaching clients prepare for a certification or license exam, I recommend they take five to ten practice tests before the real one. With GAT tests, candidates who are more practiced may perform better. Don't base your hiring decisions on any single test. All of these are informative based on verifying your interview or flagging certain areas that require more questions.

PERSONALITY TESTS

These are the most popular, tests indicating whether a candidate can fit within certain roles. For example, the Myers-Briggs Inventory can indicate whether a candidate is outgoing or introverted. It could also measure whether a recruit is goal-motivated or performs better with structure.

Personality tests also indicate whether someone is shy or assertive. These traits tend to correlate well with proactive sales ability. But these traits may not work well with a position that needs careful technical work, such as computer coding, accounting, and engineering. You don't want an airline pilot to miss extending the plane's wing flaps before landing because they are in the middle of an engaging conversation.

EMOTIONAL INTELLIGENCE (EQ) TESTS

These tests predict how a candidate builds relationships and understands both their own and others' emotions. If the position requires frequent interpersonal engagements, an EQ test may predict success.

You could also listen for EQ during the interview. For example, you may want to notice whether a candidate asks questions and whether they follow up. A good indication of EQ is the degree to which a candidate listens for emotions and can dig deeper. Your position may not require a high degree of emotional intelligence, but it's important to assess the candidate's EQ abilities.

Testing EQ is also important to determine whether the candidate is organized. One of my coaching clients asks candidates to call back the next day at 2 p.m. If they are late or miss the call, it says something about their organizational skills. If they call a few minutes early, it may indicate a level of focus that the manager feels will translate well to properly dealing with clients.

SKILLS ASSESSMENT TESTS

Earlier I suggested testing for basic math and reasoning skills. It's one thing to assume the candidate can do basic job skills. It is much better to test them during an interview. Some job boards, like LinkedIn, also test candidates before outside interviews, saving the manager time. In one commercial, the Indeed.com company displayed a candidate taking a short aptitude test.

Earlier in this book, I gave you an example of a simple high-school math quiz. Here it is again: "Jill went to the store with $10. She had to buy milk for $2.50 and a newspaper for $1 and get $5 worth of gas. She took the milk back for a refund because it was spoiled. How much is she left with?" The answer is $10 – $2.50 – $1– $5 = $1.50 + $2.50 for the milk refund = $4.

PHYSICAL ABILITY TESTS

Some positions like firefighters, police officers, roofers, and even air conditioning installers need physical strength and stamina to perform their jobs. Firemen in Charleston, South Carolina, are required to carry sixty pounds for 100 feet as part of an entrance exam. The candidate, whether male or female, is required to pass this physical test.

The US Navy Seal Team BUD/S (Basic Underwater Demolition/ SEAL) training program is really just an entrance exam for physical stamina. For two weeks, instructors force candidates to endure hard physical labor, intense fatigue, and tests of mental fortitude before they go into specialized training. If an infiltration mission requires no sleep for several days and enormous levels of stress, instructors need to know which candidates can complete it.

Similar tests are also employed in football, basketball, and most other high-intensity sports. When I played tennis in college, we were required to do wind sprints and agility drills on the tennis court long before we were selected to join the team.

An important note using any testing is the regulations enforced by the Equal Employment Opportunity Commission (EEOC). The rule states that only 30 percent of an employment decision can be based on testing. On the face of it, this is a good rule of thumb to selecting new hires. The other aspects of your selection should be based on your interviews and past employer discussions.

All these tests can inform the strengths and weaknesses of a candidate. But no single test is definitive. They should be used in conjunction with other selection tools we have discussed in this book. Most of these tests can underline and accentuate problem areas you may encounter in the future. They also may build confidence that you made the right decision.

Yet again, the way recruits performed in the past predicts whether they will succeed in the future. Testing is informative but not definitive. Use tests as suggestions to help you make better decisions.

Understanding Your Candidate's Personality

Like other tests, personality tests can be helpful, but they shouldn't be used alone in making hiring decisions. All tests can be used as tools to better understand the candidate and evaluate whether they can be successful in the position you're selecting for.

One of these is a personality profile created by Carl Jung, the famous Swiss psychologist. He was a contemporary of Sigmund Freud, the father of modern-day psychoanalysis. This early twentieth-century researcher was truly a Renaissance man. In an attempt to understand human behavior more effectively, Jung postulated that basic human behavior was driven by two parameters: assertiveness and responsiveness.

If we can understand these two behavior patterns, we can communicate more effectively. But Jung didn't stop there. He posited that if we can determine assertiveness and responsiveness, we can break human behavior down into quadrants. These quadrants then will give us a better understanding of a candidate's motivation and communication style.

When we talk about a candidate, we describe them as a go-getter, or shy, or a perfectionist. We have a myriad of descriptions and labels. Wouldn't it be nice if we could break these descriptions into four basic personality styles? Here is a way to do it. This simple assessment will help you become a better interviewer. Let's start.

The first personality dimension is *responsiveness*. This is the tendency to show emotion. Rate yourself as low or high in responsiveness. Give yourself a number between 1 and 4 on how responsive you are.

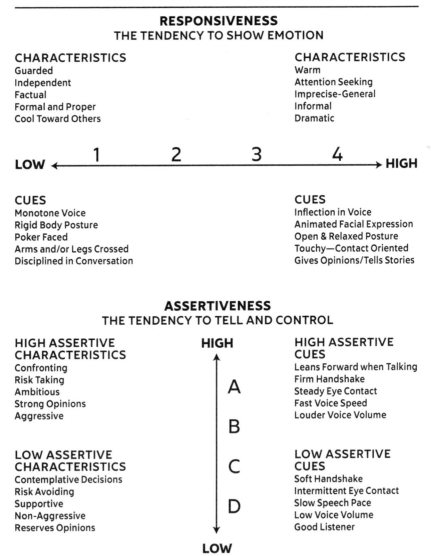

DIMENSIONS OF HUMAN BEHAVIOR
ASSERTIVENESS ⟷ RESPONSIVENESS

RESPONSIVENESS
THE TENDENCY TO SHOW EMOTION

CHARACTERISTICS	CHARACTERISTICS
Guarded	Warm
Independent	Attention Seeking
Factual	Imprecise-General
Formal and Proper	Informal
Cool Toward Others	Dramatic

LOW ⟵   1   2   3   4   ⟶ HIGH

CUES	CUES
Monotone Voice	Inflection in Voice
Rigid Body Posture	Animated Facial Expression
Poker Faced	Open & Relaxed Posture
Arms and/or Legs Crossed	Touchy—Contact Oriented
Disciplined in Conversation	Gives Opinions/Tells Stories

ASSERTIVENESS
THE TENDENCY TO TELL AND CONTROL

HIGH

HIGH ASSERTIVE CHARACTERISTICS	HIGH ASSERTIVE CUES
Confronting	Leans Forward when Talking
Risk Taking	Firm Handshake
Ambitious	Steady Eye Contact
Strong Opinions	Fast Voice Speed
Aggressive	Louder Voice Volume

A

B

C

D

LOW ASSERTIVE CHARACTERISTICS	LOW ASSERTIVE CUES
Contemplative Decisions	Soft Handshake
Risk Avoiding	Intermittent Eye Contact
Supportive	Slow Speech Pace
Non-Aggressive	Low Voice Volume
Reserves Opinions	Good Listener

LOW

Low-response people tend to be guarded, independent, factual, formal, proper, and cool or standoffish towards others. They tend to hang back before expressing opinions. They also are unlikely to discuss their own emotions and more apt to talk about the facts. They seem less engaging and have a low level of enthusiasm.

I played tennis recently with a CPA friend. One member of our doubles group told a story about a recent airline trip. I made a side comment that the example was a metaphor for life. The CPA corrected me and said that wasn't a metaphor and that I didn't understand what the word *metaphor* meant. I told him that I liked my definition. He then replied that I was living in the Dark Ages. I jokingly said that I like living in the Dark Ages. His last response was that it's better to live in the light. After smiling, I went to my side of the tennis court, ready for the match. Only a low-response, factual, independent person would have made those kinds of comments. But it's a good example of low responsiveness.

Verbal and nonverbal cues to low responsiveness include a monotone voice, rigid body posture, poker face when communicating, closed body position, and restraint in conversation. They pick out words very carefully. Henry Kissinger, Richard Nixon's secretary of state during the Vietnam War, is a good example of these traits. Kissinger still consults frequently with corporations and foreign governments. He is thought of as the oracle of foreign relations around the world. He has a thick German accent and speaks very softly and carefully. I have seen him speak multiple times without ever smiling. I have also never noticed a semblance of enthusiasm. He is the consummate low-response person.

High-response people are much different. They are warm, attention-seeking, and imprecise, and tend to generalize acts. They are informal and often dramatic. They are the people who greet you as a friend, even though you have just met. When telling stories, they may exaggerate the facts. They reason, "Why let the facts stand in the way of a good story?" They have a lot of variety and inflection in their voice. They possess animated facial expressions and are open and relaxed in body posture. They are sometimes contact-oriented. You never have to ask for their opinion, because they are more than ready to give you one with an attached story.

My brother Kevin is a good example of a high-response person. Most of the people he meets, whether in business or socially, end up as good friends. Kevin is informal and often dramatic. He tells stories that engages anybody who will listen. Just don't ask him about the facts. I've learned that you can never quite pin down his exaggerations and long ago stopped trying. Kevin will embellish for impact. He loves to liven up a story. If he listens to somebody give their opinion, it will often turn into a twenty-minute conversation. I am much less responsive than my brother. I tend to ask more questions and listen to answers. I will attend to strangers if it's an interesting conversation. But if not, I will smile, listen for a moment, and go back to what I was doing.

Are you low- or high-response? Are you guarded and independent or warm and attention-seeking? Are you disciplined in conversation or ready to give your opinion along with a story? Mark yourself as a 1 if you're low-response or as a 4 if you're high-response. If you are someplace in the middle, mark down a 2 or a 3. There are no 1.4's or 3.7's. Rate yourself in whole numbers.

Secondly, think of somebody you've had a hard time getting along with. These people tend to have opposite behavioral characteristics. What is their level of responsiveness? Rate them as well.

The second dimension of human behavior is *assertiveness*. This is the tendency to tell and control. Highly assertive people tend to be confronting, risk-taking, ambitious, aggressive, with very strong opinions. These people tend to speak before they think. They stereotypically fly off the handle. Assertive cues include a firm handshake, steady eye contact, fast voice speed, and loud volume. These people lean forward when talking and sometimes even point and touch you while talking in case you're not listening well enough. We have all met people who seem too aggressive, annoying, and sometimes obnoxious. While many of these characteristics are cultural, we tend to think of highly assertive people as an acquired taste.

I live in Portugal one month each quarter. I meet many Europeans as well as other nationalities. Yet in all my years there, I have only met five Americans. After a few beers, my British friends usually tell me what they think of Americans—all good-natured chaps, they believe: Americans are aggressive, loud, and act or react before we think. While nobody has these characteristics alone, we tend to think of these people as alpha male athletes or celebrities who believe their own brochures.

I am a professional speaker and see all kinds of high-ego presenters. After a few standing ovations, many of us tend to believe the promotional PR we put out before each speech. One of my colleagues presents in the life insurance industry. While we know each other well, I usually get a five-minute diatribe even after just saying hello. He often tells me how good his business is, the standing ovation he just got, and even how much money he makes per gig. He knows my name but very little else, since he never asks any questions. He is highly assertive. People low in assertiveness are the total opposite. They are very supportive, nonaggressive, and contemplative in making decisions. They avoid risk and often reserve opinions until they hear what you think first. Their nonverbal cues include a soft handshake, intermittent eye contact, a slower speech rate, and low voice volume. They tend to be very good listeners.

I can't think of many celebrities who are low in assertiveness, since they tend not to stand out. The best-known are highly assertive. But one noncelebrity comes to mind: my IT consultant. He is very soft-spoken and rarely makes eye contact. He is engaging as long as the topic is related to computer software or hardware. He will often talk about his adopted son, but little else. He speaks slowly and has a low voice volume. He seems to be a good listener but never makes eye contact.

Rate your assertiveness: A through D. A is highly assertive, and D indicates low assertiveness. If you are someplace in the middle, mark B or C. Again, there are no middle letters. Also rate a person you don't get along with very well. Again, these people tend to be the opposite from you in terms of assertiveness.

Your Personality Style

Let's put this all together. Circle the quadrant that corresponds to your levels of assertiveness and responsiveness. Also, put an X covering the area which best corresponds to the person you least get along with.

If you are a low-responsive (1, 2) and high-assertive (A, B), we will label you a Driver. If you are a high-responsive (3, 4) and high-assertive (A, B), we will name you an Expressive. If you are a low-responsive (1, 2) and low-assertive (C, D), we will label you an Analytical. Lastly, if you are a high-responsive (3, 4) and a low-assertive (C, D), we will call you an Amiable.

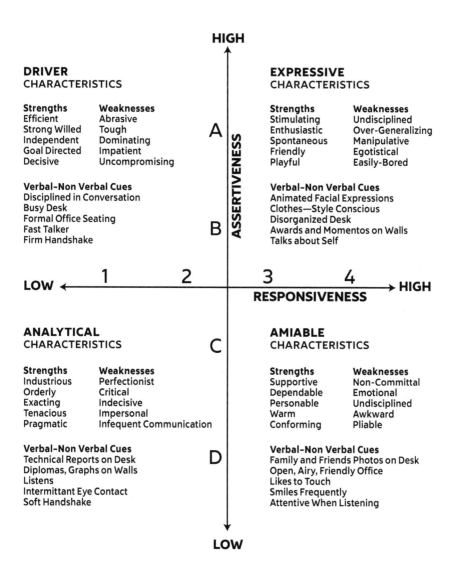

HIGH

DRIVER
CHARACTERISTICS

Strengths	Weaknesses
Efficient	Abrasive
Strong Willed	Tough
Independent	Dominating
Goal Directed	Impatient
Decisive	Uncompromising

Verbal-Non Verbal Cues
Disciplined in Conversation
Busy Desk
Formal Office Seating
Fast Talker
Firm Handshake

EXPRESSIVE
CHARACTERISTICS

Strengths	Weaknesses
Stimulating	Undisciplined
Enthusiastic	Over-Generalizing
Spontaneous	Manipulative
Friendly	Egotistical
Playful	Easily-Bored

Verbal-Non Verbal Cues
Animated Facial Expressions
Clothes—Style Conscious
Disorganized Desk
Awards and Momentos on Walls
Talks about Self

A
B
ASSERTIVENESS

LOW ← 1   2   3   4 → **HIGH**
RESPONSIVENESS

ANALYTICAL
CHARACTERISTICS

Strengths	Weaknesses
Industrious	Perfectionist
Orderly	Critical
Exacting	Indecisive
Tenacious	Impersonal
Pragmatic	Infequent Communication

Verbal-Non Verbal Cues
Technical Reports on Desk
Diplomas, Graphs on Walls
Listens
Intermittant Eye Contact
Soft Handshake

AMIABLE
CHARACTERISTICS

Strengths	Weaknesses
Supportive	Non-Committal
Dependable	Emotional
Personable	Undisciplined
Warm	Awkward
Conforming	Pliable

Verbal-Non Verbal Cues
Family and Friends Photos on Desk
Open, Airy, Friendly Office
Likes to Touch
Smiles Frequently
Attentive When Listening

C
D

LOW

Notice your own rating and that of the person you have trouble engaging with. You are opposite in your levels of assertiveness and responsiveness. In other words, the two of you have little in common behaviorally.

It's helpful to rate every candidate using this method during the interview. It doesn't matter whether your ratings are right or wrong; this is only a frame of reference.

If a colleague is also interviewing your candidate, ask what they think the candidate's personality style is. Both of you can compare notes and more effectively consider whether the candidate is right for the position. This is another tool in making good decisions about whether a candidate will adapt well to your company's culture. Again, it is only a tool. If you only have a hammer, you will treat everything like a nail. But if your tool chest is extensive, you can pick out the right one for the job.

DRIVERS

These high-assertive, low-responsive people are disciplined in their conversation and pick out words carefully. Their offices are formal, with desks and chairs arranged properly. While their desks are busy, papers tend to be organized. They talk fast and possess firm handshakes. They also get to the point quickly after only a few moments of rapport.

Strengths of Drivers

They tend to be efficient in both work and demeanor. They are strong-willed and almost certainly goal-directed. The Driver is very independent and perfectly willing to make decisions. Whether those choices are good is debatable. Decisiveness is a trait of any good leader. They will make decisions with the information at hand.

Weaknesses of Drivers

They can be abrasive and tough. Since they are low-responsive, they tend to be less concerned about relationships. They are impatient and sometimes dominating. In their quest for being efficient and effective, saying the right things can be an afterthought.

One of my clients is a stereotypical Driver. He starts out our coaching conversations with his challenges, issues, and what he accomplished over the previous week. After a few minutes of talking, he will stop and ask about my week, almost as an afterthought. He told me once that he will type a letter about the issues he wants to address. Then go back and put in the recipient's name and pleasantries, like, "I hope your day is going well." His total focus is on the goal and solving the issue. His secondary concern is the person he engages with. But this is the mindset of a Driver. You may not want one as your psychotherapist, but they certainly get things done.

Communicating with Drivers

1. After a few minutes of pleasantries, get down to business.
2. Influence their decisions by providing options and alternatives backed by facts.
3. If you have a disagreement, argue the facts and downplay emotions.
4. In praising the Driver, show support for results. Secondarily, praise them globally. In other words, praise the performance before saying how you feel about them.

In my coaching career, I've encountered all four behavioral styles. My process is to first engage the client by asking how their week went; then I ask about results. We then either review concepts or learn new skills. It's always interesting to listen to how Drivers react to praise.

One of my Merrill Lynch clients in Chicago won't accept any praise unless it's attached to results. We were working on a script of what to say to past clients. We applied an engagement technique called the five-step bridge. He wasn't getting results the first week. But since he tried, I praised his effort. He then pushed back telling me the needle wasn't moving. This is typical of a Driver. They will rarely accept praise without results. Achieving their goals first is much more important than feeling good while they're doing it.

Supervising Drivers

1. Reward them with praise for results. Tell them what their performance is accomplishing. Focus on what excellence means to their career.
2. Counsel them by being specific and factual. Engage by asking about their projects and goals.
3. Correct them by showing the gaps between their performance and expected results. Keep them focused on their goals as well as the company's.
4. Delegate by communicating the goals and expected results. But let them be creative about how they do it. Once you train them, let them find their own way of getting results as long as they are achieving what you want.

5. Reprimand by first praising their abilities, but then correcting their process.

As a business coach, I will often tell stories illustrating the concepts I'm trying to get my clients to retain. My system is: present the expected result, communicate the steps, tell an illustrating story, and ask for commitment to using the steps.

This works very well except with Drivers. I've heard more than once from a Driver, "I love the steps. This is very helpful. I can't wait to apply them over the next week. But can you shorten the stories? They take too long." Every time I hear this, I smile, thinking, "This is a typical Driver": get to the point, let's move it along.

ANALYTICALS

These are low-responsive/low-assertive people. They are comfortable with spreadsheets and technical analysis. They are often focused on degrees and certifications. They seem to appear to listen without paying attention. This is because they have intermittent eye contact and sometimes act disengaged from people. But they are engaged in the process. The overriding concern of an Analytical is being accurate. Since so much of what they think and do is black-and-white, they often argue details instead of dealing with context.

Strengths of Analyticals

They are exacting people who value details often more than results. How they arrive at a decision is sometimes better than the decision itself. They are industrious, orderly, exacting, tenacious, and pragmatic. Since they need to be right, they tend to value performance by avoiding mistakes.

Weaknesses of Analyticals

They have a tendency towards perfection. They rate themselves by how much they know and how accurate they are. But sometimes perfect becomes the opposite of good. To a stereotypical Analytical, it's better to be correct than get results. Analyticals are often critical when they hear inaccuracies from others. Because of their desire to be right, sometimes they are indecisive when they feel they have insufficient information. Relationships are tangential. Because of this, they appear impersonal and infrequent in their communication.

I am an American Airlines top-level flyer, an Executive Platinum. To achieve this level, American requires at least 100,000 miles per year and $18,000 of airfare. There is a Facebook page dedicated to this flight status group. While there are many complaints from members, we all praise individual American Airlines employees, notably flight attendants. Most of the conversations are focused on trivial details. Most of us don't engage when the conversation becomes banal. We can always determine the Analyticals in the group because they argue about esoteric details in any thread.

On a recent flight to London, I was at the top of the upgrade list. The gate agent allowed a passenger below me on the list to upgrade to a seat in business class. I posted my frustration: before the flight, the gate agent should have told me her reasoning for upgrading someone with less status. This would have prevented me becoming angry, since every passenger can see the upgrade list. One Analytical member of my Facebook group argued that the passenger below me on the list probably paid more for the ticket. Another argued that the class of service, Premium Economy, was overbooked and upgraded to business class rather than downgraded to coach. With all of these comments, you could easily see who the Analyticals were. The non-Analyticals communicated empathy without the heavy detail.

Communicating with Analyticals

1. When engaging with an Analytical, list both advantages and disadvantages.
2. Be prepared to provide proof of your arguments, using specifics and statistics while minimizing personal anecdotes. This type is more persuaded by analysis than experience.
3. Provide guarantees. Since Analyticals are so risk-averse, they need backup. If you ask them to accept more risk, such as commissions or bonuses, they will first consider a worst-case scenario.

Supervising Analyticals

1. Reward with new tools and techniques.
2. Engage by asking about the process instead of the result alone. These people are often nerdy. They are most comfortable discussing how they resolved technical details.
3. Delegate by answering all details. Analyticals are very concerned about the process and become uncomfortable when they don't know the steps to complete a task. The worst thing you can do is tell them, "Figure it out."

4. Prepare to be patient. Analyticals feel most comfortable when they have all the details. They are most stressed when they have to be creative. They may test you by asking the same question numerous times. Keep patient. Before you become frustrated with their minutiae, ask what they would do first.

EXPRESSIVES

These folks are stimulating, fun, and engaging. They are also spontaneous, playful, and friendly. They are so engaging that you may feel tempted to talk longer at the risk of wasting time.

Strengths

The strengths of Expressives include their ability to engage with anybody. They are animated and respond quickly to conversations they enjoy.

Weaknesses

Expressives seem overgeneralizing, undisciplined, manipulative, and easily bored. One of my clients manages a sales team. He always knows what to say in any meeting. The problem is that his commitments are rarely completed. When he's cornered, he reverts to how much he appreciates everybody and how tirelessly he works toward hitting his supervisor's goals. In an effort to avoid accountability, he reminds everybody on the team how many years he has worked there and how much of his life he has dedicated to the team. These are all defense mechanisms to deflect criticism.

This is a typically Expressive response to stress. They are so verbally engaging and skilled at manipulating other people that they often get their way. You may even feel guilty for confronting them.

Communicating with Expressives

Expressives talk a lot. Naturally, they love to be listened to. Because of their impressive verbal ability, it's important for you to listen to their points before making any comment.

When engaging with an Expressive, avoid details. This type will often talk a big game, but when you pin them down to specifics, they may become irritated. I spoke to one friend who fantasized about buying an apartment in downtown San Diego to rent through Airbnb. He said the space would pull in $400 per night on the weekends and $300 per night during the week. I tried to pin him down on the details. He avoided my questions and responded with, "I just know." I then called my nephew, who was doing the same thing in San Diego. Matthew said the apartment he owned rented three or four times a month for $200 per night, but it was difficult to rent during the week with any consistency.

Since Expressives exaggerate, be prepared to keep them accountable when it matters. Otherwise, just enjoy the entertainment ride. The worst thing you can do is become passive aggressive and fact check every conversation.

Supervising Expressives

These people love recognition and praise. Find something to praise, and do it daily. They also like competitive challenges. Setting up monthly or quarterly goals with motivating benefits is always a good idea. Since they crave being heard, make sure to take time to listen. But don't be swayed unnecessarily. They are good at verbal jujitsu, so make them focus on goals instead of process. Listening to Expressives may also help them solve their own problems. Earlier we talked about a useful communication technique called the five-step bridge. It's a way to "listen" Expressives into doing what you want them to do.

AMIABLES

These folks love to work collaboratively to get things done. Relationships are central to what they value in their personal and business life. They also need to be recognized by both coworkers and supervisors, so show an interest, both professionally and in their personal lives. As with Analyticals, communicate patiently, supporting them when they are stressed by confronting with the unknown.

Recently I asked my assistant Bethany to verify emails in our client list. I could tell by the look on her face that she didn't know how to start. She also looked stressed. I took twenty minutes to guide her through the process of email verifications, even though she had done it before.

Since Amiables value your interest in their personal l life, make sure you ask. A Driver might walk in the office and say good morning, never breaking stride on his way through the office. But an Amiable might think the Driver doesn't care enough to even ask about her weekend.

Strengths of Amiables

Amiables can be supportive and dependable. They are known for being warm, personable, and comforting. They could make good counselors or psychotherapists because of their great empathy. Every Amiable I have met enjoys talking about family, especially their kids. Since Drivers and Analyticals are less responsive, personal conversations with them may be short-lived.

Weaknesses of Amiables

Some stereotypical Amiable weaknesses are a tendency to be non-committal, emotional, undisciplined, non-assertive, and pliable. When an Expressive or Driver asks an Amiable to do something, they may say yes but may struggle to get the task done. For example, a Driver might ask for help with a project even though the Amiable is already overloaded. Since the Amiable tries so hard to be cooperative, they may have difficulty saying no. This may stress out the Amiable even more.

I am definitely a Driver. I will ask my staff to do projects often unaware of what they are currently engaged in. If I checked first about current projects, it would allow me to prioritize and decrease the Amiable's stress.

Supervising Amiables

Amiables aren't generally motivated by competition and incentives. But they are inspired by the chance of developing stronger relationships. You can motivate them by actively listening and drawing out their emotions. If they feel you are only focused on the goal and not on them, the conversation could be deflating.

Whenever I work with Amiables, I keep a credit balance in their emotional bank account. They have to know they are liked and valued. One Amiable employee called me a tyrant many years ago. A basic reason was not spending enough time developing our personal relationship. She simply saw me as too demanding. Every Amiable I have ever worked with has gone over and beyond the call of duty when I have spend at least ten minutes every day asking about them and their family. When I don't do that, I can create too much stress when I put too much on their plate.

Stereotypes Are Too Simple and Misleading

So far, we have surveyed Amiables, Analyticals, Drivers, and Expressives. I've given you very simple explanations for each type and its weaknesses, strengths, how to communicate, and even how to supervise. But as you know, nobody falls neatly into one category.

There are also subcategories. For example, Drivers may be broken into four subcategories:

1. Driver-Driver
2. Expressive-Driver
3. Amiable-Driver
4. Analytical-Driver

. . . and the same for the other three quadrants.

We have already explained each of the personality types. A Driver-Driver would possess all of the Driver characteristics but none of the others. An Expressive-Driver would primarily be a Driver with secondary Expressive characteristics.

As you interview candidates, use these steps:

1. First rate their predominant behavior style using the four quadrants.
2. Rate their secondary behavior style.
3. Teach this personality rating system to any other interviewers you work with.
4. Ask them to rate the candidate the same way.
5. Compare notes.

Many of my coaching candidates think a system using quadrants to determine personality is too complex. They think using their gut is much easier than trying to systematize the hiring process. Nonetheless, even if you study the personality quadrants for only an hour, you will listen better, and your listening skill is your most important tool for selecting good people.

I get pushback from coaching candidates about applying these skills. Since many have not been exposed to using psychology in sales, management, and hiring, they become overwhelmed. But I constantly explain that just applying the process makes them substantially better at picking great people, even though they are not yet experts.

I love learning languages. I took Latin and German in high school. I also became functional in Spanish. (Notice I used the word *functional*, not *proficient*.) Now that I live part-time in Portugal, I am trying to learn that nation's very difficult language. The words look a lot like those of Spanish, but the pronunciation is totally different. In most European countries, speaking the local language gets a response back in English, but in Portugal, attempting to use their language gets a smile and a Portuguese reply. You can see their eyes light up with a smile when you at least try. I've created more relationships by speaking Portuguese to my neighbors, who speak great English, than if I never attempted their language at all.

The same is true of your attempts to use these behavioral characteristics skills. Just attempting to use them is going to make you a much better interviewer. You are on your way to picking better people and retaining them longer. It all about your people skills. When you can make people feel understood, they will also understand.

4

How to Retain Great People

Recent unemployment has been as low as 3.5 percent, according to US government statistics. Yet 3 million Americans quit their jobs every month in search of something better. Shockingly, 31 percent of new hires quit within six months. This kind of turnover is severe. It costs anywhere from 66 percent to 200 percent of a first-year salary to replace a lost worker.

Many employees are mission-critical. They need to be retained to continue the viability of your business. I ate at a Japanese fast-food restaurant recently called Yoshinova. The drive-through was closed in the middle of a weekday afternoon. I asked the manager what the problem was. He said, "A few employees quit, and we can't hire enough staff right now. We had to make some sacrifices." This restaurant is part of a strong regional chain. I was surprised that hiring employees was so difficult that this store had to shutter part of its business.

Reasons Employees Leave

SALARY AND BENEFITS

You will learn later that money is the biggest reason people say they leave. It rarely is. But if the money and benefits you offer is substantially below your competition, you will likely lose staff.

Most employers' knee-jerk reaction to staff departures is offering more money or matching a competitor's offers. Employees are happy to take the extra dough but still may not stay. There are other, more relevant underlying reasons pushing employees to quit. Money seems to be a camouflage instead of the trigger.

WRONG HIRES

According to online employment advisor Glassdoor, 35 percent of recruiters expect one third of their employees to quit in the first year. Some of the responsibility for high turnover rests in the hiring process. If you see frequent job changes in an applicant's résumé, expect a short stay at your company as well. Often during the hiring process, we rationalize why candidates left their last job and why they will be successful long-term with us. While this can happen, expect the past to be prologue. How a candidate behaved in the past is likely the behavior they will display in the future.

Earlier in this book, I mentioned why it's important to evaluate the candidate's strengths and weaknesses using the eleven key questions. It's also important to sell the position. Getting a candidate excited about a job is important in building their motivation. Unfortunately, many hiring managers go too far. They sell the good parts of the job and don't communicate the negatives.

One of my coaching clients hypes new candidates. He talks about the mission and core values of his company and how important the new position is in helping everybody hit their goals. He talks about his one-, three-, and five-year plans and about how excited he is to find a candidate who will help everybody in the company achieve their objectives. When he finds a qualified candidate, he goes one step further. No matter how excited the candidate is in accepting the position, the manager makes sure the negatives are communicated as well. Only after the first interview will he give reasons why the candidate should not accept the position.

Sometimes the candidate is so romanced that they ignore the negatives and want to accept the job anyway. In any case, my client will never accept yes for an answer. He will schedule another meeting no less than three days later to give the candidate a chance to sleep on it. He wants to downplay the romance of a new job. This is all an attempt to not only hire the right people but retain them. It may feel good to hire a qualified person. But losing them in six months would be a greater pain than the joy of filling the position right now.

Wouldn't it be wonderful if we could pick life partners this way? I met my wife, Merita, on a blind date. In 1989, an American Airlines flight attendant friend flew from Santa Ana, California, to Chicago on a DC-10 with ten flight attendants on board. My friend Karen asked all ten to gather in the aft galley. She immediately separated the married women from the singles. She asked each single lady a series of questions about their likes and dislikes. I told Karen what I was looking for. One by one, the flight attendants were dismissed, leaving only Merita.

Three months went by. I finally called. Merita was delightful on the telephone and even more engaging during our noncommittal cup of coffee. This was our lead-up to the first date. I was thirty-five and she thirty-three. Both of us had been in terrible relationships and were ready for someone nice. It was love at first sight for me and an expectation of hope for her.

If this were a hiring interview, I would have told the candidate the pros and cons of the job. I would also want the candidate to tell me the same. But at no time during that first date did I tell Merita that I was sometimes arrogant, narcissistic, easily bored, and a workaholic. She also failed to tell me that she was absent-minded, disorganized, in debt, and unable at the time to resolve conflict. Although we have been married thirty-one years so far, in many ways we were flat-out lucky to stay together so long.

It's great to have a first date result in infatuation, followed by a second date where the whole truth comes out. Hearing the truth too soon may have caused Merita to walk away, as could I. But during our one-year courtship, knowing the negatives could allow each to look for patterns of behavior to prove or disprove what we were each warned about. We were lucky to get the right person. Don't depend on luck when you pick new recruits. Tell them the positives up front, followed by the negatives later. If we can prepare candidates for the negatives, as we should potential romantic partners, perhaps each would be retained longer. Anything we can do to get good employees past the one-year mark is worth it.

STRESS AND FRICTION

We can't expect employees to be motivated when they feel uninterested. When staff feel overworked and disregarded, they look for anything that can release the stress. When that doesn't come readily from you, the employee may look for new opportunities. Often more money alleviates friction, but not for long.

Some of my clients assign annual sales quotas. They often demand that staff work long hours under stress to hit their numbers. Many will treat staff to vacations or bonuses for a job well done. But others will continue the end of the year pressure much longer.

You have read that my wife, Merita, is a flight attendant with American Airlines. These crews have been stressed over the years by a loss of benefits, bankruptcy, retirement plan changes, and even higher healthcare costs so the airline can stay profitable in a competitive industry. A few years ago, Doug Parker, then CEO of American Airlines, offered the benefit of two positive space airline tickets anywhere in the system as a way of saying thanks. (Positive space is a confirmed seat, whereas a nonrevenue is stand-by space. Nearly all airlines offer standby space to their employees. But rarely do they offer positive space.)

While this was generous, the stress of frequent delays, canceled flights, union contract conflicts, and illness produced by toxic uniforms was overwhelming. As a result, American Airlines saw many flight attendants and pilots leave. In addition, Covid pressed the airline to offer early retirement for most flight attendants and pilots over the age of fifty-five. American now has a severe pilot shortage and will have to pay much higher salaries to retain current pilots. If the employees feel valued, they will take care of the customers. But that is rarely the case. Doug Parker's stated that his values were, employees first, but American is the least profitable airline among the big three. When employees feel friction, any operation will suffer. And costs will go up.

You should always be looking to alleviate areas of friction. When an employee complains about an issue, be sensitive to others who may feel the same. I have over forty years' experience advising small business owners. I have rarely seen irrational employees. For the most part, they work hard and want to produce a product or service to the best of their ability. When you see friction, it's critical to solve it immediately.

POOR LEADERSHIP

Many people want to be bosses, but very few people want to put in the effort to be good leaders. One of the biggest reasons people leave a company is the supervisor. There could be personality conflicts, irrational expectations, or just a lack of appreciation.

You can probably remember an employee who complained about their supervisor. One of my friends told me recently he should have started his own company ten years ago. His boss is impossible to work for and never shows any appreciation for the work that is done. A British friend in Portugal recently turned sixty. At his birthday party, he displayed a picture with his boss. My friend made the boss millions of dollars. I asked if it was worthwhile. He looked up and said, "Maybe." He also could have responded that it was a waste of twenty years of his life. Neither would be a ringing endorsement.

The better leader you are, the better people you will retain. The better your people do, the more money you will make. The worse you are as a leader, the more costly everything will become. Here are some things you can do immediately to become a better leader instead of just a boss.

Leaders communicate goals and future direction. Bosses don't.

Leaders let employees know where a company is headed and set benchmarks to get there. Bosses tell people what to do without giving them any clear Idea of why they are doing it. Leaders communicate a mission and shared values to get there. Leaders share objectives with their team. They celebrate success with the whole team as often as they can.

Leaders handle challenges and offload stress.

Bosses produce stress. When a problem or issue comes, leaders help employees through the issue. Bosses put blame on their employees in order to disguise their own lack of effectiveness. Leaders help teams solve problems so the team can be better. I have always told my team it was my job to clear the obstacles out of the way so they could run their fastest.

Leaders value employees; bosses value metrics.

Leaders try to develop employees and support them even as they pursue personal goals. Bosses are focused on the numbers, not on what it takes to get there.

Many years ago, I worked as a consultant for an insurance company in Orange County, California. The salespeople were instructed to cold-call for three hours a day in an attempt to book two face-to-face appointments. Some of these thirty salespeople hit their goals within an hour or so, but they were still required to cold-call for the full three hours. I asked the owner of the company to reward those who could book appointments so quickly. One way to do it was giving them the morning off with pay when they booked two appointments. But since the owner was a boss, not a leader, he wanted the salespeople to put in the time regardless of the results.

Leaders build confidence. Bosses beat employees up emotionally.

Good leaders help employees become competent and confident by allowing mistakes to happen. Bosses reprimand employees for making mistakes. Bosses often make passive-aggressive comments when those mistakes occur.

Scopely, a Los Angeles–based mobile gaming company, actually encourages mistakes. They realize that a learning company thrives and grows by encouraging employees to take risks. Jason Weiss, the former general manager of Scopely, said that failure isn't just tolerated, it's celebrated. At the end of each week, Scopely holds a "failure of the week" competition. A member of each team shares their most epic failure and what they learned from it. In this way, teams within the company can learn from other teams.

Compare this to Amazon. The company has a "bruising" culture, as described by *The New York Times*. A *Times* reporter spoke to former and current employees, who said the experience of working there was intense pressure, unreasonably high expectations, and constant backstabbing from colleagues. The median tenure at Amazon is only one year. Think of the cost and time in hiring that Amazon HR staff must endure. If this were your company, could you afford the expense? Jeff Bezos is consistently among the top five richest people in the world. How much better off could Amazon be if it developed better leaders?

According to *The New York Times*, one of the most egregious systems within Amazon is the Anytime Feedback Tool. This communication platform enables any employee the ability to provide feedback about fellow colleagues directly to that worker's manager, but it is all done anonymously. The tool was created to collect both positive and negative feedback. All Amazon employees are ranked, and poorly rated employees are terminated. The tools are often used by employees to sabotage one another. Negative feedback is often used as a reason for withholding promotions, pay increases, and merit benefits without feedback from the targeted employee. The Anytime Feedback Tool has contributed to an atmosphere of fear and mistrust, underlying a major reason for the high employee turnover.

Compare this to American Airline's Someone Special program. Every elite flyer is given ten of these coupons to reward any employee who has displayed customer service over and above what is required. Each month, the president of American Airlines draws these coupons and awards ten recipients $10,000 each. While the likelihood of anyone winning is about 1/10,000, the recognition is impressive, especially since employees are also given the Someone

Special coupons as a way of saying thank you. They can also give each other these pieces of recognition, which are eligible for the drawing as well. While I have been an American Airlines top-level Executive Platinum flyer for more than thirty years, I have much to dislike about the airline. But Someone Special is a program that helps retain employees. While it is unlikely that any employee will win the drawing, recognition from passengers is always a good way to show appreciation and make employees feel good about their jobs. In this way, they are likely to stay longer with the company.

Lack of Support

This is a big reason why good people leave. This can be something as simple as an outdated computer or a lack of help from colleagues. My daughter Stacey left a job many years ago because she wasn't getting support from her boss, a US congressman. Stacey was chief of staff and managed sixteen people. But the congressman wouldn't support her. He said he did not want to get involved in staff problems. Not supporting your team is a quick way to lose them.

Support isn't always a matter of authority or emotion. It can also mean logistics. A computer that's five years old and breaks down can undermine support. One of my coaching clients wanted to take a team of top producers out of a branch office because the air conditioning system was uncomfortable. In addition, there weren't enough photocopiers. What irritated him the most were the paper-thin walls in the cubicles. He didn't feel his colleagues could use the telephone to sell because everybody in the office could hear everyone else's conversations. He complained to the branch manager several times, but the complaints never resulted in change.

Earlier I mentioned that leaders reduce friction instead of create it. When there is a problem with a supervisory office, leaders run interference. If there are changes to be made, leaders will help employees in the process. This is another form of support. Leaders stand up for their people and support them. If you can't support an employee for any reason, either you or the employee may need to change.

Lack of Training

This is one of the biggest reasons why the under thirty-five-year-old cohort leave a company. At twenty-five, I worked for Kidder Peabody, a financial brokerage company. They offered to reimburse tuition expense for an MBA program. I applied and was accepted into the executive class at Pepperdine University. I was really excited, but a month before class started, Kidder discontinued the tuition match. I quit the company within three months.

One of my clients trains all new hires to be investment advisor representatives. The Series 65 license to earn the IAR is difficult at best. Only 56 percent pass the test. But my client puts new hires through an intensive training program, earning them a license they can use the rest of their lives. While there are continuing education requirements associated with the license, a series 65 license makes them more valuable to any future employers. This is the kind of training the under-thirty-five crowd loves. In fact, this could be the deciding factor between accepting a position at your company or a competitor.

How to Train Anyone to Do Anything

Training isn't just external. You can provide some of the best training yourself. The problem is that many leaders don't know how to train. They think that instruction should be done by telling people what to do. That is not training; it's only direction. Great leaders train effectively and help employees learn lessons they can apply and retain.

Four steps to train anybody to do anything:

1. **Communicate the significance of what you are training them to do.** Often managers tell people what they want them to do. As a result, people don't really master the skill. They will do what it takes to please the instructor. Consider the military basic training sergeant. What if he tells a recruit how to dig a foxhole and walks away? They recruit does the minimum and digs a four-foot foxhole. The sergeant then tells the recruit he died from a grenade that penetrated five feet. The significance is survival during a firefight. It is not digging a hole just because the sergeant told you to do it.

2. **Show them how to do it.** Always show people how to do a skill. If you don't know how, get someone else to demonstrate. Some of the biggest mistakes I made as a coach was telling my clients what to do without showing them how to do it. If I haven't mastered the skill, I can't expect them to become an expert either.

3. **Watch them do it.** No real learning comes without role play. If you're teaching somebody a computer program, you need to watch them do it. If you're showing them a sales skill, they need to

role-play in order to master it. I role-play with my clients every skill we cover. Clients who feel confident that they know a concept will make mistakes when we do it together. It is surprising how little they remember to implement. Always role-play. Let your employees show they have mastered the skill.

4. Wait a day, and watch them do it again. During my graduate studies at the University of California, we tried to figure out how memories were encoded in the brain. Memories are actually made up of engrams, much like a packet of information that travels over the Internet. The difference between it and the human brain is the Internet forgets nothing and the human brain remembers little. There's a lot of research from electrical brain stimulation studies showing that memory is much more retentive than previously known. In fact, over 95 percent of what we see, hear, and feel is stored. The problem is, we can only retrieve about 10 percent over the long term. We are unable to retrieve 70 percent of what we see, hear, and feel within one day, and 90 percent within three days. One of the ways you know memories are stored forever are your dreams. In dreams, you may be able to access in detail events that occurred years ago but you have largely forgotten while awake.

Therefore, 10 percent of what you teach an employee today will be retained after three days. If you want a skill or a training concept to be retained, wait a day or two, and role-play again. Spaced repetition works much better in helping the mind retrieve information than just teaching people once. You may get a few groans and moans, but they are more likely to retain information if you retrain and role play again.

LOCATION

My oldest daughter, Stacey, worked as a press secretary for two US congressmen and the governor of Virginia. She got her start in politics as an intern for ABC News under Sam Donaldson, a former evening news anchor. After working on the Hill for many years, she joined a lobbying group based in Washington D.C. She was recently recruited to Park City, Utah, as a communications executive for a large resort-based company. The money was the same. There was no real income difference between the two jobs. In fact, she really enjoyed her job in D.C. But she is an obsessive snow skier. I taught her to ski when she was five years old. Since then, we have skied in Chile, Argentina, Canada, and even New Zealand. Like many young professionals, she left not because of the money but because of the opportunity to ski and raise my grandchildren in an outdoor living environment.

Retain Employees by Being Available

Managers often talk about an open-door policy. A laissez-faire manager will only speak to employees to correct behavior. A leader will engage. You don't have to become best friends, but friendly engagement always pays off. People leave managers, not companies. Chances are that if you ask someone why they left their last job, they will talk about the person they were working for, not their compensation.

One way to keep employees is using positive engagement. In one Gallup poll, 56 percent report being somewhat engaged, and 73 percent report being actively disengaged and are looking for a different job. The answer is consistently and actively trying to engage your staff.

Daily Information Protocol (DIP) Engagement Tool

One of the best ways to engage employees is through an approach called *daily information protocol* or DIP. If you want to fully engage and recognize your staff, meet with all of them three times a week. This is typically a standing meeting in which you ask each three questions:

1. What did you get done yesterday?
2. What is your goal today?
3. Here is my priority for you today.

The brilliance of this approach is its brevity and engagement. You are meeting with all of your staff on a frequent basis without wasting anyone's time. Each of your staff learns what the others are doing and becomes appreciative of their duties. You also get the chance to praise great work and give positive direction to those who seem less engaged. If you need to correct or reprimand, do it alone. If you reprimand people in front of others, they will sabotage you behind your back.

Staff also have the tendency to silo, or focus on their own activity without recognizing the efforts of others. When you do DIP, others on the team learn the difficulty of other jobs and appreciate their efforts. You also get the chance to celebrate minor successes during each meeting.

But keep each meeting short—no more than fifteen minutes. Don't let employees digress. If you allow DIP events to extend, the team will resent the distraction from their own tasks. If there is a conflict, be flexible in allowing team members to miss these sessions on occasion. But communicate privately how important the meetings are to other members of the team and how much cohesion means to helping each other.

Above all, celebrate success. If any member of the team makes progress, praise them. It will encourage others to achieve in order to be praised also.

One of my clients, Matt, owns a mortgage company in Salt Lake City, Utah. He flew me into speak one day to a real estate group. That morning I was able to see him conduct a DIP meeting with ten of his staff. They all gathered around his desk, standing and listening to each other for about fifteen minutes. As he listened to what each employee accomplished the previous day, he found something to praise. As he listened to their goals for the current day, he was able to add ways to be more productive, such as which files to prioritize.

Matt is a very strong leader with wonderful communication skills, but at times he is too overbearing. He tended to tell employees what to do instead of asking them how to do it. Whenever you engage your employees and discuss objectives, always ask what they would do before you give instruction.

A learning environment helps people become independent. It also allows people to make mistakes. If your staff thinks that you have all the answers and never fail, they will ask for your advice on everything before doing anything. This is the opposite of delegation. You are trying to make people self-sufficient, not dependent. You're trying to develop and engage people and make them more productive, not allow the job to be robotic.

Advanced Exit Interview Techniques

It's critical to do an exit interview with every worker who leaves your employ. Whether you terminate or they quit for another job, find out what made the position difficult as well as effective. This will help you choose the right traits and characteristics in your next candidate. This will also increase your chances of hiring successfully the next time.

Many years ago, my top salesperson was recruited by a competitor. I was disappointed and irritated that she had such little loyalty. I swallowed my pride a week later and asked why she left. It wasn't because she wanted more money; it was due to a conflict with another on my staff. The staffer challenged and often berated her because paperwork wasn't done well or on time; it was also often inaccurate. The traits that made her a good salesperson were also those that the detail-minded staffer couldn't stand. After learning this, I fired the administrative person and hired a new salesperson, who was even more successful.

One of my coaching clients did exit interviews on salespeople who quit. He learned that many couldn't stand the rejection. Xerox research showed that a typical sale incorporates an average of four rejections before a yes occurs. So, in his search, he decided to interview for tenacity and perseverance. He was really interested in salespeople who would go an extra round to get the sale.

In one of his first boxing matches, Muhammad Ali, then still known as Cassius Clay, was emblematic of going one more round. Early in his career, he was matched with Sonny Liston, the best boxer of his day. In the seventh round, Cassius was getting pulverized by Sonny. Liston was three inches taller and had a four-inch longer reach than Clay. When the bell rang, Clay went to his corner, ready to quit. But he had a secret weapon by the name of Angelo Dundee. Dundee said, "Go one more round. Liston is hurt worse than you are. He is about to give up." Cassius Clay started taking his gloves off when the bell rang. At that moment, Dundee pulled the stool out from under him, which meant he couldn't sit down, gave him a wedgie, which meant he had to stand up, and even kicked him in the back, which caused him to take one step forward. At that moment, a towel was thrown in the ring from the Sonny Liston side. He quit the fight. Cassius Clay won. The rest is history. I saw the match on video many years ago. If Cassius Clay had not gone one more round, he would not have become arguably the best fighter in boxing history.

How to Do a Stay Interview

Exit interviews don't often yield enough information to answer the question of why people leave. Many employees don't make it past the one-year mark. Yet hiring managers assume the reasons are benefits and money. According to *The Wall Street Journal*, Columbia MedCom, an eighty-year-old medical communications company, dramatically decreased turnover. Before the intervention, the turnover rate had increased from 13.4 percent to 19 percent in a total staff of fifty-eight. The prime pool of new recruits consisted of college graduates. But twentysomethings are known to hop around their first few years after college.

Columbia tried to find out what made employees stay. The company conducted a series of face-to-face informal interviews with employees having at least three years of longevity. The questions were:

- Why did you come to work here?
- Why did you stay?
- What would make you leave?
- What issues do you consider nonnegotiable?
- What would you change or improve in your manager's behavior?

Not surprisingly, senior management discovered the glue that retained many long-term employees was the people they worked with. Employees who stayed more than three years also valued flexibility in scheduling and personal time off, as well as opportunities for internal promotion and development.

Columbia MedCom now pays more attention to individual development plans in order to help each employee reach their goals. But the real benefit of the stay interview is to gain information about how to retain good people. It is better than the superficiality of an exit interview, because departing employees just want to leave. The stay interview helps employees improve their work life.

Advanced Retention Techniques

During the interview section above, you read about the "let's assume" technique. This is a very effective tool in getting candidates to imagine themselves three years in the future and look backwards from that perspective in an effort to tell you what they want. This allows them to tell you the three things that are most important in selecting a new position. When you find out what those three things are, you can keep those goals in mind in developing new employees. When you can develop employees and focus on what they want over the next three years, they will stay with you. Remember, money is rarely the most important reason people leave. Friction with other employees and a lack of opportunity and development may cause staff to look elsewhere.

The "Let's Assume" Technique in Retaining Great People

The same "let's assume" technique can be used in getting people to stay put. Just as you use the three steps in interviewing candidates, the same skill can be used in retaining them. Since we know candidates tend to leave a position between six months and one year, you should do a performance review three months after the hiring date and continue every three months from then on.

1. ASK THE QUESTION. LISTEN. DON'T INTERRUPT.

Ask, "Let's assume it's three years in the future. What happened that let you know it was a great place to work and you had a great manager?" Since any good interviewer is looking for three goals, it will be very tempting for you to interrupt and sell the opportunity. Bite your tongue and be empathetic. If you interrupt, you won't hear any other goals. If the employee has nothing to say, you can prime the pump. You can offer possible responses to get the conversation going. But don't let them just mirror back your words. Give them time to think and be candid.

2. QUANTIFY THEIR EMOTIONS.

Often employees will talk about emotions like happiness, income, and quality of life. It's up to you to make these tangible and measurable. A way to do this is to ask, "What does *happiness* mean to you?" Keep drilling every emotion down until the candidate gives you a number. Will it be a certain balance in their 401(k) plan? Will it be a 20 percent increase in salary? Will it the ability to be home by six o'clock in order to spend time with their family? Will it be a promotion to more responsibility in the company? Will it be developing more valuable skills?

Bottom line: make their goals tangible and measurable.

3. RECAP AND TRIAL-CLOSE.

A recap is restating the other person's words. According to one study, 86 percent of people were persuaded more effectively by feeling understood; only 4 percent were persuaded by being made to understand. A recap helps employees feel understood. An example is, "If I heard you correctly, you said you wanted to gain better sales skills, increase your income by 35 percent, and at some point get promoted to regional manager. Did I get that right?"

A trial close gets employees to commit to a solution. It uses the words, "If we can . . . , would that be valuable for you?" Or, "If we can take a look at . . . , would that be a benefit?"

For example, "If we can work toward helping you develop better sales skills, increase your income by 35 percent, and rise to regional manager in the next three years, would that be something we could talk about and work toward?"

Now you know what will keep an employee in their job over the next three years. Their goals may change. But if they do, replace the goals when you do performance reviews. It's the trial close that causes people to commit and emotionally buy in.

Applying the "Let's Assume" Technique

Let's assume that during the interview the candidate was interested in learning more about spreadsheets, increasing their income, and contributing more to the company. Let's also assume that you drilled down the spreadsheets objective into being proficient at Microsoft Excel. Increasing income was defined as a 10 percent bump in salary. Contribution meant sales increased.

During the performance review, you would ask how they were progressing towards their mastery of Excel. You then would ask if they were on track to making a 10 percent increase in salary based on their improved performance. You would finally ask how they were contributing towards the company's sales.

It's very easy to assume what an employee wants. But those desires may not be consistent with what you think they should focus on. Only when you can put the employee's goals into concrete terms will you know why people quit. It's unlikely that staff quit only because they received a better opportunity. It's much more probable that they quit because they are not achieving their goals and have become dissatisfied.

One of my coaching clients headed a mortgage company with ten employees. His office manager quit suddenly, also taking the loan processor. My client attempted to do an exit interview, but there was no benefit for the manager. She just said, "I found a better opportunity. You are wonderful. Thanks for all that you've done. But I'm moving on."

This was a worthless exit interview. If my client could have initially done a stay interview, including the "let's assume" technique, every three months and reviewed three goals consistently, the manager may have stayed. Employees don't leave good jobs they enjoy because of a better opportunity. They leave jobs when they are not hitting their goals and have to suffer through bad relationships.

Unique Ways to Retain Great People

A lot has been written about retaining good people. Installing pool tables and beanbag throw games in an office seems to appeal to any millennial or Gen Xer. Some companies like Big Spaceship, a strategy, design, and technology consultancy in Brooklyn, also have unique employee retention ideas. Big Spaceship allows employees to bring dogs to work. The appeal of having a dog at your desk seems serene. The negatives might come when two dogs get aggressive and start barking during key client meetings.

Hyatt Hotels, McDonald's, and Starbucks often hire entry-level people. Since some of the most important goals of twentysomethings is training, Hyatt offers one-off classes and training sessions from Khan Academy, an online training platform. Starbucks and McDonald's offer tuition reimbursement programs that not only retain but attract key people.

Outsourcing Until You Find Great People

We discussed earlier the challenge of finding great people when so many have left the workforce. Whether it is the Great Resignation, a worker shortage because of childcare challenges, or a greater than expected retirement of those over fifty-five years old, we still have to run a business.

Through the techniques discussed in this book, you know that recruiting is a constant process instead of a job to engage in only when you need someone. Many companies are filling vacant jobs by outsourcing. Full-time employees are expensive. You need to train and pay employer taxes as well as benefits. Often healthcare, sick leave, and vacation benefits amount to one third of the annual salary. But contractors and professional service firms don't come with those expenses. The more unique the skill set needed, the more expensive contractors become. Applying the one-third cost of benefits, these expenses can be commensurate with what you would pay a full-time employee without the commitment.

Another benefit of outsourcing is quality control. It's much easier to terminate a consulting agreement than a full-time employee. In my practice, a coaching client often works with me for a year or two and stops, but then reengages with me after a hiatus. In a way, I am their outsourced consultant. In fact, 60 percent of all my coaching clients at some point will return to coaching. Our outsourcing agreement gives them the flexibility that using me as a full-time employee would not.

There are several types of outsourcing roles available. One is the typical 1099 consultant, who is engaged by you but also has other clients. They could be paid by the project or, in the case of sales and marketing, a commission. In many situations, they can also work directly in your office.

Another outsourcing example is a virtual assistant. Phone calls can be directed to this person and then forwarded to you if necessary. Administrative paperwork can also be handled by these workers. Many of my colleagues use virtual assistants in the Philippines, India, and other countries with English-speaking staff. These assistants are paid to send marketing proposals, design brochures, and even schedule and confirm meetings. Many speakers like me depend on virtual assistants to send books and audio-video products to buyers attending meetings.

There are many sources of consultants, virtual assistants, and 1099 workers. Many use Fiverr. This is a professional outsourcing site offering various services from virtual assistants to graphic designers. Any outsourcing job you can imagine can be found on the site. I post social media messages on LinkedIn three times a week. The social media/graphic designer is located in Albania. She does a wonderful job at very low cost. Another consultant sends email newsletters to a few thousand subscribers. If your business is growing, you may be able to afford a full-time employee. Most of us need only a couple of full-time employees, utilizing outsourced consultants and virtual assistants.

Sometimes I hear the objection that the outsourced consultant needs to be licensed or certified in some way. Possibly they need to have an accounting degree or a license demanded by a regulator. This is not an obstacle to outsourcing these duties. It only means you may have to pay more for the consultant and possibly take more time to find someone.

I have mentioned that it's important to hire slow and fire fast. The worst thing is not hiring the wrong person, it's keeping the wrong person too long. This is not the case when you outsource. It's much easier to fire a consultant and hire a new one than fire an employee. Unless you have a consistent and predictable need for a full-time or part-time employee, start with outsourcing first. If you lose an employee, consider outsourcing before you hire somebody new. It may be that you never needed a full-time person at all.

Hire Only A-Level Players

Netflix is a good example of how to retain great people. From shipping DVDs in the beginning to later online streaming to producing award-winning videos, Netflix has been able to disrupt the entertainment distribution industry. But their talent retention strategy is also impressive.

They hire only A-level players. Besides foosball and free sushi, Netflix HR executives believe that hiring the best people is the ultimate perk. Great people like to work around other great people. You rarely hear winning Super Bowl championship players talk about how bad their teammates are. When a World Series winner is interviewed, they often talk about the brilliant skills of their teammates. Once in a while, a sore loser will talk about how bad the running game is or how their baseball pitching bullpen let them down. But winners love to have winning teammates.

Netflix keeps great people for other reasons too. They treat employees like adults. Many companies have an expense policy in which every expenditure requires a receipt. (In fact, many companies require prior approval otherwise there will be no reimbursement.) But Netflix has a five-word expense policy: "Act in Netflix's best interest." They trust employees to do the right thing. This policy treats valued employees like adults. But Netflix has always been innovative. They offer a one-year paternity leave for new dads in addition to maternity leave for moms. Their travel policy is, "Travel as if it were your own money." My favorite is the Netflix policy on the use of company resources. Their attitude is, "Take from Netflix only when it is inefficient to not take, and inconsequential." They explain this as, for example, making personal phone calls on a work phone when it is important to do so. Or printing personal documents on Netflix equipment when it would take too much time away from your job to go to a printer. These common-sense policies retain employees.

During the 2021 NFL season, Tampa Bay wide receiver Antonio Brown took off his jersey, threw it up into the stands, and walked off the field in the middle of a game. Officially, he did this because of an injured ankle. But before his shocking departure, he was recorded yelling at his fellow teammates, and there were reports that he was upset at their play. Injuries occur in every sport, but they are usually handled well. Injury or not, Brown's performance was not that of an A player who uplifts the level of his team.

Working with A players is challenging, instructive, and engaging. It is also a more enjoyable work environment for everybody on the team. Insistence on surrounding top people with top talent is a key driver for any team's retention.

Why Employees Stay

One of the best ways to recruit is to retain. The longer you can keep great people, the less often you will have to hire. Depending on the position, it costs on average $32,000 every time you lose an employee. If you combine that with lost production and training time, that number gets even higher. The best part of recruiting is retaining. It's also the easiest way to recruit. According to Harvard research, there are five reasons that cause people to quit.

But first, here's a question. Where would you put money on the list? First? Second? Although it is often the reason a candidate decided to work for you, money is dead last as the reason your best people leave.

FUN

The biggest reason why staffers thirty years and younger leave is, "It's not fun around here." When my daughter Stacey graduated from college, she introduced me to a fellow student raised in Southern California. I needed an administrative helper. I quickly hired her and was impressed with her ability and skill. After three months, she left to work for Enterprise Rent-A-Car. She said Enterprise had employee beer parties on Friday nights and treated top performers to weekend sports events. It was more fun than working for me.

Make the Job Fun

There are many ways of making the job fun. It could be as simple as having a pool table or foosball table in the office. It could even be a basketball hoop in the parking lot. Often companies will organize sports pools, including betting on the game of the week. But innovative managers will also use personal incentives, such as giving administrative people time off for getting a project done. Making the job more fun is really all about the creativity of the leader. It is less about grand gestures, like taking employees to a basketball game, and more about doing small things every week to make the job more interesting and enjoyable.

My youngest daughter, Caroline, once worked for a golf club in San Diego. The general manager took many of the staff to Nashville, Tennessee, for a "training retreat." Yet the only pictures I saw were of the attendees drinking, not training. I'm sure the training retreat was well intended. When Caroline returned home, I asked what she learned in Nashville. She said only that there was a difference between silver and gold tequila.

Weekly Competitions

One of my clients in Des Moines, Iowa, holds a weekly competition for sales goals. He offers early Friday departures when his people hit their recruiting goals. This costs the manager nothing, but it's very motivating. One of my other clients offers an early departure day when a salesperson hits their goals. My client would rather they hit goals in three hours, even though he's paying for eight.

Some companies try to attach fun to performance in other ways. They offer premium parking spaces for perfect attendance or a free lunch for anyone who hits their goals. While these are more incentive-based, any competition can be fun. My golf club offers premium parking spaces for tournament winners.

RECOGNITION

Many who leave say they are underappreciated. They feel they work very hard, but nobody notices. This is critical when working with salespeople. I once wrote a magazine article entitled "The Maladaptive, Irrational Cognitions of the Super Sales Producer"—a funny title underlining a very serious issue. Top sales producers don't work for money alone. They tolerate rejection and objections because they want other people to recognize them. They want to be noticed.

If you want to keep great people, praise them three times every day. You are probably thinking, "They don't do things worth praising." The rule of thumb in praising is give recognition at least once per day. You don't have to wait for perfection to praise. You can actually motivate people to become better simply by communicating praise and recognition. Have you ever noticed how trained animals seem so talented? The answer is a psychological concept called *successive approximation*.

Successive Approximation: How to Motivate People

When killer whale Shamu performed at Sea World, handlers didn't wait one day for Shamu to jump a hundred feet in the air through a fiery hoop. They successively approximated the target behavior over many months. The first day they fed Shamu a fish for poking its nose out of the water. The second day they would put a fish in the middle of a hoop on top of the water. The third day they would put the hoop one foot above the water with a fish in the middle. This training would successfully approximate the end result by bringing Shamu closer and closer to the hundred-foot jump.

You can use the same tactic to improve performance. For example, an employee consistently arrives at work thirty minutes late. You can either wait for them to be on time or praise and motivate them toward the goal. Let's assume, for example, that they are aware of when the workday starts. When the person comes in only twenty-five minutes late, he gets praised for being earlier. The next praise would occur when they were twenty minutes late, followed by fifteen, then ten, then five, and finally coming in on time. This method will modify behavior, but you have to couple it with praise.

It may seem more straightforward to set expectations and demand performance. It also seems easier to stand in the doorway of the office, tapping your watch when the tardy employee arrives. While reprimand and criticism can stop bad behavior, these tactics do nothing to motivate people to perform better. You might be able to tell a poorly performing salesperson that they will be fired unless production increases. But isn't it more motivating in the long run to praise people into better performance instead of punishing them?

The Hawthorne Effect: Attention Motivates People

In the 1950s and 1960s there were football fields of typists and clerical people at Western Electric's Hawthorne Works in Cicero, Illinois. Day in and day out, these workers were robotic in their duties, mainly thinking of their next Caribbean vacation or what they would do on the weekend.

An experiment was conducted at this plant. When a light bulb blew out, maintenance workers put up a ladder and changed it. Managers noticed that productivity increased by 7 percent within view of the repair. Time and motion specialists (which is what industrial psychologists were called in those days) were curious. Why would a light bulb increase motivation? One bright PhD replaced a totally functional light bulb in another area of the building. Productivity from those workers increased by the same amount. He realized that it was not more light that increased motivation, it was attention. This is now known as the Hawthorne Effect.

This is what praise does. When you notice people and pay attention in a positive way, motivation increases. Leaders continually attempt to develop their teams. But not many are able to develop people who want to improve. Everyone wants praise. There are very few employees who don't respond to it. In fact, the more you praise, the longer you will retain.

Three Steps to Praising People into Better Performance

Here are three steps you can use to praise people into performing better. Raising ability and motivation isn't only about pay and material reward. It's also about how much the employee wants to improve. The silver lining is that the more you praise, the more enjoyment you will create in the workplace, and the longer you will retain great people.

1. Praise people in front of others. Everybody wants praise. Nearly every performance study shows that praise is often more valued than a raise in pay. When you praise people in front of other people, others will also do more to receive the same accolade. Praising in front of other people also raises the morale of those who hear it.

Many years ago, one of my clients refused to praise his people because he said they didn't do anything praiseworthy. I convinced him to give it a shot. On our next coaching call, he said, "You can't believe what happened this week. I did what you told me and praised people multiple times per day within earshot of the rest of the office. At least three people over the next week told me the office seemed more fun lately. Something changed; they didn't know what. They felt the whole office was more uplifted and motivated." The morale of the whole office improved simply because he was praising people in front of others.

2. Praise the behavior first. Often leaders will say, "Good job," or "Nicely done." While this makes people feel good, it does nothing to increase the frequency of good behavior or improved performance. When you praise, be very specific. For example, praise people for extra activity, using a specific communication technique, or reacting positively instead of giving up. You can also use successive approximation, praising people for simply being better than they were yesterday.

If you want someone to feel good, just say, "Good job." But if you want someone to improve performance, praise them for a specific behavior they did well or at least improved. My wife, Merita, told me many years ago she was able to praise me into coming home earlier in the evening. After work, I would often play tennis in the late afternoon and get home about 8 or 8:30, late for dinner. This would make her crazy, since she wanted to have dinner together with the whole family. Instead of getting mad, she would tell me what time she wanted me home. Then she would praise me, at first for arriving earlier, and eventually for being on time to dinner. She modified my behavior. She motivated me to be on time. That's what praising a specific behavior does. When you praise people for a behavior, you get more of it.

3. Praise the whole person. While praising behavior causes replication, praising an employee in general creates motivation. After you praise someone for a specific action they did well, praise them again globally. For example, praise them for the behavior you want them to repeat. But then say, "You're doing a super job in this company. We're lucky to have you here. Keep up the great work." Through these general praises, you will get an employee not only to continue a specific action but to feel good about themselves and you in the process.

Above all, try to praise your people at least once per day. Motivation is like a bank account. Praise is a credit; friction is a debit. Your employees often feel friction during the average day. We need to increase the credit balance in the bank account with praise. Praise retains your good employees. When their emotional bank account has a debit, they start looking for another job. It's as simple as that. If you forget your daily praise, don't load it up on the next day. It will seem disingenuous. Just catch yourself and become disciplined enough to open your mouth and catch people in the act of doing something right.

Touching to Increase the Impact

If you really want people to remember a comment, you will tap their arm below the elbow as you praise them. Research from the University of Minnesota has shown that any comment you make can be remembered 300 percent longer with a touch. I've already told the story of the server who sold a tray of tequila shooters with this technique.

I recommend that you try this tactic socially before using it professionally. The rules of unwanted touch are simple: If someone says, "Don't touch me" or stares after a touch, stop. If they notice the touch, you are doing it too long. It should be just a tap.

How to Reprimand

Reprimanding employees is never easy. It's much more fun to praise. But when you need to reprimand, it's critical to do it effectively. The rule of thumb is to never reprimand in anger. Always reprimand when the person needs it. Not when you are so angry that you can't hold it back. Most importantly, make sure the reprimand sticks. Make sure the employee takes it constructively. The recipient needs to learn and raise their performance. Here are three steps to reprimand in a way that causes people to perform better.

1. Always reprimand people alone. Often managers will reprimand when they feel angry. They hold emotions so long that they explode. Sometimes the explosion occurs in front of other people. But nobody likes to be embarrassed. Nobody likes to be diminished in front of others. If you reprimand employees in front of others, they will sabotage you behind your back.

Thirty years ago, when my marketing director failed to hit her numbers, I got angry in front of two administrative people in my office, who were very good friends with her. After the reprimand, I went to lunch with a client. I came back to an empty office. They had all quit. The administrative people immediately took her side and complained about my poor behavior. Instead I should have closed the door and calmly told my marketer what my expectations were and exactly what she had to do to achieve them.

2. Reprimand the behavior, not the person. Reprimands go wrong because the employee feels diminished, slighted, and personally attacked. They blame you instead of themselves for the issue. This is because reprimands are usually focused towards the employee instead of the behavior. For example, "You made a mistake on the case that failed." Instead, the reprimand should have been, "A mistake was made on the case that failed. What can we do to prevent that in the future?" In other words, instead of blaming your employee, acknowledge the behavior and brainstorm how it can be prevented. Then finally get their commitment to implement the change.

For example, "Proposals need to be followed up on within twenty-four hours, especially in competitive situations. Will you call clients from now on within twenty-four hours after we send out proposals?" If you try to correct the behavior instead of the person, they will take it constructively. If they feel you are blaming or singling them out, they may instead blame you for being a bad leader.

3. After any reprimand, praise the person globally. Not everybody can reprimand elegantly. A way to ensure that an employee takes a reprimand constructively is to praise them immediately after you correct a behavior. For example, "We need to send proposals out within twenty-four hours, especially in competitive situations. Will you do that within twenty-four hours from now on? You are doing a super job for us. Were lucky to have you. Thanks for trying so hard in everything you do. I really appreciate you and your hard work."

No rational, even-minded person would walk away from a reprimand like this without feeling good about themselves. They will correct their behavior. At the very least they will realize you are being fair and simply doing what you think is best for the company. If you don't make people feel good after a reprimand, they will not only fail to correct behavior but blame you afterwards.

The answer is to catch them in the act of doing things right. Successively praise them for improvement. Praise them for doing things better than before. If you want someone to complete tasks better, praise them for improved effectiveness.

Don't make "perfect" the enemy of "good."

This is also called *behavior shaping.* One of my coaching clients said he started praising his salespeople every day. At the next sales meeting, fifteen of the salespeople brought him a cup of Starbucks coffee and said how much better they felt working for him. None of the salespeople knew why. They just felt morale was higher. You can actually create higher performance by praising people three times per day.

The Five Reasons Candidates Join a Company

You just learned why people leave your company. Why do you think people join? The reasons may be different than you think. Accordinging to the same Harvard study I mentioned about, employees are attracted to your company based on five reasons, in this order:

1. MONEY

Most hiring managers appropriately think money is the biggest attraction for a new candidate. While this may be true, prospective new hires have nothing else to compare. They don't know how good your company is. They don't yet know anything about management commitment, vision, mission, or dedication to staff.

Since every recruiter talks about their commitment to staff, statements often become rhetorical.

A critical concept to keep in mind is how much to pay a new hire. Rarely do candidates pick a job based on an increase in salary. What they want most is to avoid taking a decrease. If you could pay somebody what they made in the last job, it will give you room to increase their salary based on future performance. I'm sure there are exceptions. One includes a candidate who is severely underpaid. But generally candidates are happy to start with what they currently make with a promise of an increase in the future.

My son-in law Benji was offered double his current compensation. A new facial recognition startup in the Bay Area was looking for an executive who could jump-start the organization. The plan was to sell the company or go public within five years. Benji was much more focused on taxes in California and what it would take to move his family than he was on the income increase. He also wasn't convinced that the technology was competitive enough yet. Moreover, when he looked at the income increase taking into consideration the higher taxes in California, there wasn't a big difference in income between his current job and the new one. Money for my son-in-law wasn't even in the top five. Don't be fooled when you hear candidates brag about a new job with more money. It's often not true.

2. FUN

This is one of the most important decision points for a millennial or Gen Xer. When everything is equal, they want to have fun at their job. It could be anything from retreats, casual office recreational activities like ping-pong and bean bag games to a Friday afternoon party.

3. TRAINING

This is also one of the most important decision points for a Gen X or Gen Y candidate. They are hopefully looking ahead ten years in the future. Especially between the ages of twenty-five and thirty-five, candidates are attracted to training that is transferable to other jobs. If you can point them to the training your company provides, it could be a factor even more important than a slight increase in salary over their last job.

In a recent issue of the *Harvard Business Review*, the University of Madeira showed that 5,000 Portuguese workers considered employer-provided training comparable to a 17.7 percent net pay raise.

4. SUPPORT

This could be a wide range of benefits, including a new computer system, work environment, and even the comfort of a workspace. Generally, support means that your staff has the tools to do the job. It could be fast Internet, social media presence, or even a typing platform that prevents carpal tunnel syndrome.

In a remote working environment, support could mean more flexible hours, a faster Internet connection, a gym membership, lunch delivery expense, or even child care. There are a lot of ways to support a remote worker. I personally think a Pandora or Spotify membership playing soft jazz all day would be a great support gesture.

Of all the ways to retain key staff, making the work environment productive is the cheapest.

5. RECOGNITION

You probably remember that people want to be appreciated. You also know to recognize effort beyond the call of duty. But frequently companies take an attitude of "just do your job." This laissez-faire mindset is not good for motivation or making people feel appreciated.

Recognizing performance above and beyond is not enough. It's important to recognize any performance that even meets expectations. This is one of the reasons why people stay with your company.

Of course, candidates don't know yet what recognition or support they will receive, since they haven't worked for you yet. But they will rate recognition high after a few months.

You probably know that people want to be appreciated. You also know to recognize effort beyond the call of duty. But frequently companies take an attitude of, "Just do your job." This laissez-faire attitude is not good for motivation or making people feel appreciated. We've already discussed how to use praise-based reward systems to change and motivate behavior.

Recognizing performance above and beyond is not enough. It's important to recognize any performance that meets or even exceeds expectations. This is one of the reasons why people stay with your company.

As you read earlier, American Airlines' Someone Special program gives top-tier flyers ten recognition coupons every year when they qualify for status. The cards typically have a place to write in the employee's name, flight, date, and a description of the great service. But aside from passenger approval and recognition, American's ground and flight crews pay little attention to getting these. A drawing is done every month for $10,000. Any employee who gets these cards will send them to Dallas to be included in the quarterly drawing. There are thousands of these cards submitted for a relatively small amount of money. You are more likely to win the California lottery as you are winning $10,000 from American Airlines.

My wife, Merita, has been a flight attendant with American Airlines for nearly thirty-eight years. She submitted the Someone Special cards for years and eventually gave up. Every time I fill out a card and give it to a deserving American Airlines staff member, they are always appreciative, but behind the smile, there is no real reward from American Airlines. If I give a flight attendant a Someone Special card for helping me find overhead baggage space, she feels good. He feels appreciated. But the quarterly drawing has little impact on her motivation to improve performance. When a reward is meaningless, it has little effect on the behavior it means to improve.

So, there you have it. These are the five reasons why people join your company and also why they leave. It's not enough to know why a candidate will join your firm. You also need to know why they leave. The better part of hiring is retention. If you can keep good people, you won't have to hire as frequently.

5

Conclusion

Your ability to recruit, hire, and retain great people is the most valuable business skills you will ever possess. Without them, your business will never thrive. You learned that because of the aftereffects of Covid-19, there is a lot more demand for workers. Many over fifty-five workers will retire permanently, or they will reenter the workforce in a more flexible fashion. They may want to set their own hours, or where they work. They may want to take vacations when they want and include more time with family. You need to also be creative in recruiting these folks on the cusp of retirement.

You also need to be more open to ad hoc gig type or workers. Hire short-term staff for a specific project instead of a long-term employee. This will allow you also to find good people you want to keep longer.

Chapter 1:
Why Finding Great People Is Critical

You learned why a low unemployment rate forces you to improve recruiting skills. You also learned why many new recruits quit within six months while others don't make it past the one-year mark. You learned that great talent must be recruited. It's possible to mold a piece of clay into artwork. But as George Raveling, the great college basketball coach, once said, "It's better to find a diamond in the rough and just shine it up."

You learned that a high percentage of your candidates are not qualified. You could spend weeks searching for a good candidate, or use innovative techniques like virtual voice mail. This is a way to listen for energy and past performance during voice mail playback instead of taking weeks to find someone worth interviewing.

You also learned that job posting services such as ZipRecruiter, Glassdoor, Indeed, and others filter keywords, but not much else. They rarely screen for the unique characteristics you need. So putting in key phrases into your job posts will serve as a good screen no matter where you advertise.

Your website and social media presence indicates your brand and is in effect your first interview. Your brand needs to be understandable and consistent with how your employees and customers see you. If your brand is about employees, it's critical to feature them throughout your website.

You learned the key characteristics of a website with a solid brand. Candidates will research you and your company before an interview. Your brand had better be attractive. You learned six things a brand is and how to create your own. Later in the chapter, you read about questions you need to answer in building a brand. Branding comes in two flavors: what the company means to customers and what it means to employees. Meshing those two statements together in a meaningful and consistent way is important. It's also the beginning of creating your mission and values message.

Part of your job is being able to communicate your brand. You learned how to create an elevator speech that causes candidates to want to learn more. Finally in this chapter, you learned that hiring for experience is no assurance of getting somebody good. As with divorce and remarriage, you may be just trading problems.

Chapter 2: Where to Look

Where do you look for great people? In this chapter, we covered five basic areas for finding good people. We also talked about the difference between passive and active candidates. Active candidates are looking for a job move right now. Passive candidates, who may be better, are persuadable but are not actively looking. To find the passive candidates, you should use nominators: people in your network who may know good possibilities.

It's important to create a list of good candidates. Then keep in personal contact every three months. The biggest mistake any recruiter will make is waiting for a job opening to start the recruitment process. You should be looking on a consistent basis.

Another way of developing this list is asking your current staff for referrals. In this section, you learned how to incentivize them to suggest a constant source of good people.

Often recruiters don't know what to say to passive candidates. The worst thing you can do is ask if they are looking for a job. The best thing you can do is use the five-step referred candidate script, utilizing your elevator speech.

Often passive candidates will report they enjoy their current position. They aren't looking for a job. But while 69 percent of candidates would like to change jobs right now, 83 percent would consider a new opportunity. It's up to you to find out what will motivate them to make the change. To engage these passive candidates, we covered a technique called the *wedge*. This is a way to find out what candidates really want over the long term and whether they are hitting their dreams right now. If you can help them progress towards their goals faster than the path they are currently on, you may be able to start a more productive conversation. To use the wedge effectively, we discussed three steps that allows you to listen instead of pitch. You also read a step-by-step dialogue on exactly what to say and how to respond.

The book is focused on how to recruit, hire, and retain great people. But you should also be willing to fire people who haven't worked out. Leaders often make the mistake not of hiring the wrong people, but of keeping them too long. One third of your employees could and probably should be terminated. You've worked to develop and give them many opportunities, but you still can't get them to perform at the level you want. Instead of creating friction and replacing them, you have avoided termination and learned to live with mediocre performers. This is another reason why good recruiters should consistently look for good people.

Chapter 3: How to Interview

In this section, we focused on the five biggest hiring mistakes you can make:

1. Rationalizing poor behavior. When people show you who they are, you should believe them.

2. Hiring experience and skills. Hire attitude first, skills second.

3. Pitching the candidate instead of listening. Selling and hyping a candidate is a sign of a recruiter who doesn't know how to interview.

4. Hiring friends and family. It's tough to train and potentially fire family members.

5. Not going enough with your gut. Hire with both your head and your heart.

Another mistake you will make is not realizing candidates often have more experience interviewing than you. This is especially true with active job seekers. They may interview between five and twenty recruiters who all ask basically the same predictable questions.

Remember that 73 percent of résumés have inaccuracies, exaggerations, and even lies. You need to immediately spot when the candidate is fabricating the truth. Although you can't confront a candidate directly, you can dig deeper into details surrounding their responses. You learned how the FBI spots lies by the way suspects move their eyes.

You also learned the three basic perceptual and communication patterns candidates display. From NLP research, you learned how to communicate with a candidate in the way they want instead of the way you want to communicate with them.

A critical part of the interview process is the eleven key questions. Since most recruiters interview subjectively, the hiring process is based on their personal opinions. But if you can ask questions objectively, evaluating good and bad answers, you will be able to predict future behavior more effectively. In asking the eleven key questions, you learned how to assign a numerical score to responses. This way you can compare one candidate against the other using an objective metric.

You learned about emotional intelligence and how important it is to listen between the lines during an interview. Since the current culture is coarser than twenty years ago, we talked about interview etiquette. Candidates can also become customers. It's important to interview well, no matter what the outcome. You are also supporting your brand and possibly creating a customer relationship.

Both interviewers and candidates sometimes stall. In other words, they don't have the ability to say no. It may be because they don't know how to be direct. When the candidate isn't interested in your job opportunity but won't tell you, you will waste time trying to follow up. Conversely, when an interviewer will not be direct, it is waste of the candidate's time. To prevent this, we discussed the upfront close. In other words, say yes or say no, but don't say maybe.

Some candidates are overqualified. Interviewers often jump to the conclusion that such candidates may not stay, but there are many reasons why they may be willing to take a job below their abilities. It could be reemergence in the workforce, a desire to spend more time with family, or even a goal to decrease stress.

Above all, listen and probe well enough to find out why the over-qualified candidate is interested in your position.

In a low unemployment economy, some candidates will accept the position but not show up. The under-thirty-year-old candidate may not know how to confront an issue and instead just avoids it. In this section we discussed five questions you can ask to make sure the candidate wants the job and will show up. We also discussed what to do when they don't show.

There are several biases nearly every interviewer has. Many of these deal with appearance and age. You are likely to make the mistake of judging people in the first four minutes. But this may prevent you from finding good people. Always hire slow, fire fast. No matter how desperate you are to fill a position, replacing a hiring mistake is worse.

There are three kinds of evaluations you should use with a new candidate.

1. Their résumé.
2. Their interview performance.
3. Their past performance.

Among the three, past performance matters most. If you can't talk to past supervisors, you are taking a risk. Past performance accounts for 50 percent of your ability to choose great people. Sometimes supervisors don't want to talk to you. They are under the mistaken view that it is illegal to discuss a past employee, but the only legal constraint they could be liable for is slandering a past employee. We discussed exactly what to say to past employers in order to get their candid appraisal and personal opinion. The past employer is critical in informing you whether the candidate will succeed.

We also discussed the notion that people don't change. The past is prologue. How people behave in the future largely reflects how they have behaved in the past. Since past performance matters so much, your ability to evaluate it is the best indicator in predicting future performance. We discussed exactly what to say to gain this information.

Preemployment testing is a major consideration in hiring good people. Unfortunately, too much emphasis can be put on these tests at the risk of diminishing your own interviews and evaluations from past employers. These tests consist of:

1. Job knowledge
2. Integrity evaluation
3. Cognitive ability
4. Personality
5. Emotional intelligence
6. Skills assessment
7. Physical ability

To help you evaluate candidates more effectively, we also discussed segmenting personality based on two dimensions of human behavior: assertiveness and responsiveness. In turn, we broke those into quadrants. We labeled the four personalities as:

1. Drivers
2. Expressives
3. Analyticals
4. Amiables

It is simplistic to stereotype anyone. But separating candidates into personality styles allows you to communicate differences, including strengths and weaknesses, with others. We also broke these pockets of personality into subcategories to make your evaluations more accurate. We all label people as "nice" or engaging," but it's a lot easier to let another in your organization know that you just interviewed an Amiable, for example. Or you could say that the candidate may be an Expressive, but you are interested in what your colleague thinks about them. This tool helps you use personality characteristics as a touchstone for communicating your impressions about the candidate.

As you try to analyze these traits, you will not only evaluate people more effectively but also engage and supervise according to the way they want to be communicated with.

Chapter 4: How to Retain Great People

The most important part of hiring is retaining. Aside from the time it takes to hire somebody new, the cost of losing an employee can be anywhere from 66 percent to 200 percent of their annual wage in finding a good replacement. In addition, 30 percent of new hires will quit in the first twelve months.

The most common reasons employees quit include:

1. Salary and benefits
2. Constant bureaucratic friction
3. Poor supervisory leadership
4. Lack of support, technical and otherwise
5. Lack of training

6. Poor frequency and quality of communication

7. Location

Many managers think exit interviews produce useful reasons why people leave, but departing employees usually aren't interested in being candid; they just want to leave. It's much more effective to do a stay interview while they are employed than an exit interview when they leave.

Companies that retain people consistently work toward hitting employees' goals, but first you have to know what those goals are. To achieve that, you learned how to use the "let's assume" technique in a different way. Initially used as an interviewing technique with new candidates, you learned how to use this skill with existing employees to find out what will make them stay. Used effectively, this could be one of the most important tools helping you retain great people.

We spoke about the top reasons people join a company and the top reasons they leave. Most departing employees will tell you they left because of more money. While that may be a factor, departures are more often based on the supervisor's lack of leadership skills. People don't leave companies; they leave managers.

One very effective way of retaining good people is to motivate them. One of the major reasons people stay with an organization is recognition. You can use praise to not only retain good people but motivate them to perform better. These steps are:

1. Praise people in front of others.

2. Praise the behavior first.

3. Praise the whole person.

In applying this three-step process, we also discussed how to build better performance incrementally, using successive approximation. In much the same way that animal trainers build behaviors, you can build performance in your employees without paying more money.

Correcting behavior is difficult and challenging. Most leaders don't reprimand at all or do it impulsively. When you need to reprimand, it should be done infrequently and never in anger. A reprimand should always be to correct the behavior of someone you want to retain. If you don't want to retain the person, look for their replacement. In this section, we discussed the three steps of a constructive reprimand instead of letting resentment be the outcome of the process.

We also outlined a four-step learning process outlining how to train anybody to do anything. Most of the time, managers tell people what they want them to do. Because we forget 70 percent of what we hear after one day, and 90 percent after three days, simply hearing instruction will be quickly forgotten. These four steps will allow you to train anyone at any time without waiting for a class to attend.

You now have better skills at recruiting, hiring, and retaining people than 95 percent of other managers. You're likely to learn only a fraction of this information working for larger corporations. It's even tougher to learn these skills as a small business owner. But now you have a step-by-step process to run your business more effectively. Your most important job is hiring great people. Every successful leader reports their business would never have been successful without hiring, training and retaining great people.

I recommend that you go back to the beginning and reread this book. Mark it up with a yellow highlighter. Make copies of pages like the eleven key questions and keep them on your desk as a reference tool. As a successful leader, you will use these skills and techniques on a daily basis.

If you have any questions or comments, please contact me at:

www.KerryJohnson.com

Kerry@kerryJohnson.com

Twitter: @DrKerryJohnson

Facebook: DrKerryJohnson

Phone: 714-368-3650

CPSIA information can be obtained
at www.ICGtesting.com
Printed in the USA
JSHW041806240622
27098JS00001B/1